# This Ain't No
# PRACTICE LIFE

*A blueprint for living a life of*
*passion, purpose, and intention*

Micheal J. Burt

# MAXIMUM
## *Success*

"A leadership consulting firm that helps people
and organizations realize their full potential"

www.maximumsuccess.org

# This Ain't No
# PRACTICE LIFE

## Copyright © 2007

ISBN: 978-1-59872-893-4

Layout and design: Sherry M. Wiser George

Editorial Assistance: Cathy Lower and Mitzi T. Brandon

First Printing: June 2007

Printed in the United States of America by InstantPublisher.com

For more information, visit:www.maximumsuccess.org

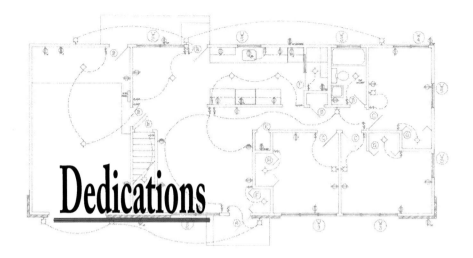

# Dedications

To my 2007 State Championship basketball team
for teaching me to believe and for practicing the
contents of this book.

To Janet Morris. Thank you for making me realize that one
only becomes a leader when he practices what he preaches.
Thank you for helping me develop my spiritual self.

To John Henderson. You've been the
greatest stepfather a son could ever have.

To my mother, Melanie Henderson. You are my rock.
Please continue to urge me to chase my dreams.

To Mitzi Brandon for helping make this a reality.

To Colby Jubenville for the opportunity to teach at the
collegiate level and share my message with future leaders.

Contact Micheal today to book your next
transformational experience!

Maximum Success
www.maximumsuccess.org
2746 Stonehedge Drive
Murfreesboro, TN 37128
coachburt@comcast.net
615.849.2099

## Maximum Success

*Speaking to, consulting, and working with organizations to create an environment of enthusiasm and action toward significance.*

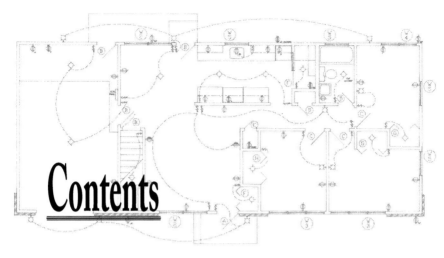

# Contents

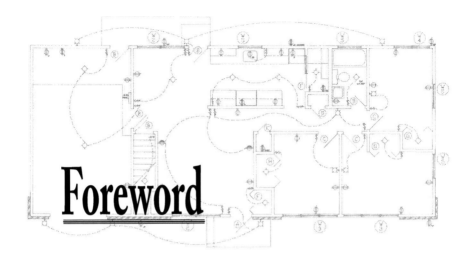

# Foreword

It was something I constantly thought about while reading this book. How does one understand life in the terms of practice? It may seem foreign to some, but Michael's point is well taken. How we practice translates into how we play. But play what? What is the play? Do you have a play? Can you call a play or change a play at the line of scrimmage?

I think the ultimate answer revolves around meaning. Yes, life with meaning is what Mr. Burt is on to. But, what gives life meaning?

When I thought of practice the first image that painfully bubbles up were my high school football August practices and then even more painful were my college playing days at Millsaps College in Jackson, Miss.. It was at Millsaps that I first was exposed to what Michael discusses in his book.

Millsaps was a seamless experience of social, physical, and mental pursuits that provided a foundation of meaning:

meaning that gave the ability to view how processes in life are tied to end results. As I look back on my experience there, it was the greatest practice field one could ever imagine! Education was not compartmentalized, but rather, intersected at a place called meaning.

Did I understand that then? No. And as life has continued to evolve with family and professional accountability as well as relationships with the need for this sort of foundation the need along with solutions became even greater.

We live in a world where we are stretched to the point that we become blurred to the boundaries of life. Boundaries, in all we do, help define purpose and provide focus. Essentially, we are stretching to the point that we no longer question, we simply do.

We are told at a young age to compete and win, and we don't know why. We are pushed to go to school, to get more education, to make money and at the same time never stop once to ask why? Why do I exist?

I continually asked myself that question as I progressed though my life's journey; especially as I moved into my master's and doctoral work at Southern Mississippi in Hattiesburg, Miss.. Life at that time, was in some regards about trying to gain academic pedigree rather than gaining substance but at some point all of us have to ask about the capacity for which we seek.

That capacity is simple: to be counted. To be known for something. To in the end, have someone else peer into your life and say, his time here was well spent.

Before you read this book, write that down and as you go through chapter by chapter list the meaningful moments in your life. Were they sport related? Family related? Business related? Team related? Individually related?

Lloyd Gray, a graduate from Millsaps and the editor of the *Northeast Mississippi Daily Journal* wrote in an essay in a Millsaps alumni magazine, "Learning how to make a lot of money and learning how to make a life are two entirely different things..." At one point in my life I probably agreed.

But as I have met people like Michael Burt and my colleague and advocate, Dr. Ben Goss, an assistant professor in the College of Business at Missouri State in Springfield, Mo., we subside to a different way of thinking. Thinking in terms of "What are the elements of a life well lived?" not entirely about outcomes, but about process and experience and how they impact outcome.

Ben, Michael, and I have all lived in a time period where economic prosperity has never been greater and the fallout continues to grow. As we all sit charged with educating people this has never been more apparent. We live in the age of guarantees, point and click, and zero accountability. By virtue of our own success we have lost our way. But all is not lost.

If you find yourself struggling with these questions this book is for you.

If you find yourself saying, my boss, wife, husband just does not address the real issue, this book is for you.

If you are a coach and you have parents, players, teachers, and a community waiting for the world to change, this is for you–AND THEM!

Finally, if you, right now, standing where you are, say why am I not the person I want to be? Smile, shake Mr. Burt's hand, have him sign the book, and begin reading–today. When you are done, hand it to someone you care deeply about and ask them to do the same.

Can the world be saved? From who or what and with asking the right questions–maybe, but, only if we will take the time to turn the camera around and take a picture of ourselves. This book allows you to do that.

What do I owe myself? What do I seek individually and collectively? What are the elements of a life well lived? Or, as singer songwriter John Mayer states,

> *One day our generation, is gonna rule the population, so we keep waiting, waiting on the world to change. Not Coach Burt, not me, and hopefully not you!*

**Colby B. Jubenville, Ph.D.**
Coordinator, Sport Management Program
Middle Tennessee State University

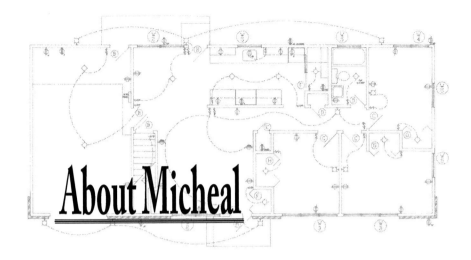

# About Micheal

Micheal Burt has one goal in his interactions with his clients—to transform and impart knowledge and skills to improve the current condition of the people and the organization. Through years of leadership and personal growth study while pursuing his doctorate of management in organizational leadership, Micheal has learned what works and what does not. With a philosophy deeply scripted in building the "whole person" then building the entire group, Micheal will help you make the transition from where you are to where you want to go.

Through short stories, humor, and intensity Micheal will walk you and your organization step by step through a sequential process of finding your unique voice in life to inspiring others to find their voices. Through cultivating the process of vision, discipline, and passion tied to a worthy cause, Micheal will help illuminate and validate the worth and potential of you and your people and awaken the internal motivation of the organization. The author of three books on personal growth, leadership, and coaching, Micheal's deep-rooted background in education and practice as a leader of a large organization adds to the experience of the presentation and will leave you with the tool set and skill set necessary to create action and enthusiasm toward significance.

Micheal has worked with people of all ages—high school, colleges, and corporate America—to help people and organizations optimize their resources and reach their potential. A client list includes Tennessee Health Care Association, Bristol Regional Medical Center, Middle Tennessee State University, Dell, Inc., Cornerstone Health Care, The National Beta Club, Murfreesboro Medical Clinic, Virginia Woodall Sports, TennSight, FirstBank,and many others.

Micheal was named one of the "Top 40 Under 40 Most Influential People in Tennessee" in 2004. He enjoys leading one of the top athletic programs in the state as the athletic director and head women's basketball coach at Riverdale High School. In 2007 he led his women's basketball team to the highest honor in Tennessee by winning Murfreesboro's first state championship in 83 years. In addition, he is an adjunct professor at Middle Tennessee State University in the department of Health and Human Performance. His books *Changing Lives Through Coaching, The Inspirational Leader,* and *This Ain't No Practice Life* can be purchased through his Web site, www.maximumsuccess.org.

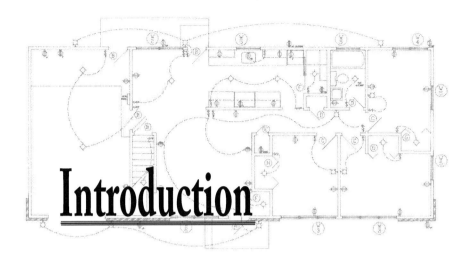

# Introduction

More than six years ago I began to speak to groups as part
of the coaching profession. After a speaking engagement at
a banquet one evening a man came up to me and said, "You
should really go on the speaking circuit because you have a true
talent for speaking." His words lit a fire in me that continues
to burn even stronger everyday I live. That day I began to
sense that God had given me a talent to inspire others with
words and light their fires so that they could go and act on the
hopes and dreams in their lives. Albert Schweitzer once said,
"In everyone's life, at some time, our inner fire goes out. It is
then burst into flame by an encounter with another human
being. We should all be thankful for those people who rekindle
the inner spirit." As I continued to hone the craft of oration, I
began to sense a much deeper hunger in my soul that said I was
put here to help others find their voices in life. I began speaking
at every opportunity I could and became a regular in a college
class at my alma mater, Middle Tennessee State University. As
I began to deliver my message each class, I grew and began to

realize the message I was delivering centered on several major themes and those themes centered on passion, significance, meaning, and execution. I began to title my presentation *This Ain't No Practice Life*. I chose that title after my newly found premise that the ultimate success of one's life is measured by how she invests her time in a cause that she deems worthy and significant and how much she impacts others along the journey. Two years passed and my passion for inspiring a larger group continued to resurface, much like the gnawing at your conscience that many feel when something keeps telling you there is a bigger world out there for you to impact. Hungry to learn, I attended an Achiever's Circle offered by speaker and small business owner Mark LeBlanc in the spring of 2003. My fire was reaffirmed and validated. At the end of that Achiever's Circle, Mark encouraged each participant to stand up and give three minutes of their best stuff. I was the youngest and most inexperienced speaker in the room but I gave it the best I had. The title of my presentation was *This Ain't No Practice Life*. Once completed I braced myself for scrutiny and critical words from the other participants, and especially Mark. He looked me squarely in the eye and said these profound words that have stuck with me. "Micheal, if you don't write a book on that concept then it is nobody's fault but your own." Man, that was powerful!

Leadership can be defined in some circles as affirming someone else's self-worth and potential so much to them in so clearly a way that they begin to see it in themselves. That day I found my voice and know deeply that I am here to help as many people as I can to find theirs. That is my mission in life and the deepest need for writing this book.

In the summer of 2004 I wrote my first book *Changing Lives through Coaching* to help leaders formulate a vision for working with others and acting on that vision. It outlined my holistic approach to developing each player from a body, mind, heart, and spirit paradigm and a method for tapping into the full potential of each constituent. I followed up with a spin off of that book titled *The Inspirational Leader* which outlined what I felt was a gap between how people wanted to lead and how they were actually leading and focused on leading others through inspiration and validation. I deeply enjoyed the writing process of both of those books as it was both therapeutic to me and I hope to those that read them. It was during that writing process that I did exactly what I urged others to do and that was connect with some of my real passions in life and act on my thoughts. Even during that process I knew there was a greater theme, a theme for all people—not limited to just coaches and leaders. That deep, burning desire led me to this book and to reach out to touch as many people as I could. The word inspire means to "breathe life into" and ultimately that is what I think we are all searching for. Your situation may differ from others, but deep within your inner core is a longing to do something that matters with your time and talent and to find the sweet spot of your life. From my experiences as a head women's basketball coach, an athletic director, to a speaker and consultant communicating to people all across the United States there are a couple of common threads that intertwine everyone. Those threads exist at one's deeper core of conscience that urges us to connect to our source, find our meaning and purpose, and live a life in service to people and causes in which we believe.

As I traveled the country speaking to virtually thousands of people of all walks of life on topics such as personal motivation, leadership, effective team building, and finding their passion, I found a common denominator: a need to live a life of passionate execution and significant contribution. People really do want to wake up in the morning knowing that their lives do affect others in a positive way and that they are connected to a cause they deem worthy. The other concept I've noticed throughout my travels is a gap that is present between what people really want out of their lives and the results they're getting. What I've found between that space of that wonderful mental creation many people have and the physical act of creating it is usually a litany of excuses or perceived roadblocks. For whatever reason, people only act when there is enough pain or enough potential, otherwise they just stay put and watch the days go by. My hope is that this book will reach thousands of people and breathe life into them and give them the push they need to act on their thoughts and to truly write the program for their lives, and more importantly live that program. I was speaking at a management seminar in New York when it occurred to me what I actually do for a living. *I help people go from where they are to where they want to go. I illuminate and validate the potential in others in so clearly a way that they begin to see it in themselves.* Pretty simple, huh? But boy, it is powerful when executed. Anyone can make a living, but only the strong can make a life. What does your life represent and what is your purpose here?

I also found through my travels another common theme among people that was apparent everywhere I went. We will all face some level of adversity in our lifetimes. To what degree we face will be unclear to predict but how we use that adversity to accelerate progress will ultimately determine our level of significance in the world. In the end, between stimulus and response YOU always have a choice to how you respond. If you can change the picture of viewing adversity as a negative experience to one of learning, growing, and changing then you view bad situations as life's greatest teachers. In this book, we'll take a look at exactly how to do that.

Today is the day to get off the mat, get rid of the excuses, and begin to build a life that matters. People don't regret what they do in life; they regret what they don't do. This book will include a road map to navigate you through life and help you get where you are going along this sometimes tumultuous journey. Follow the process, enjoy the ride, and promise yourself that you'll make every second count. I've designed this book in a way that you can challenge yourself daily. The contents are built around *seven keys to personal and professional significance* and serve as the means to unlock *seven doors to your happiness and fulfillment.* I discovered these seven keys while traveling the country speaking to people from all walks of life. If you are not a big reader take one challenge per day and make it a 90-day process. By the end of the book if you act on the content I believe you will see a tremendous transformation in your life. The good and positive will begin to manifest itself in a way you have never experienced before because all seven keys are centered on taking ACTION. To help illustrate my points I've included *The Belief and Action Model,* which entails the process of *Believing, Seeing, Doing, and Reflecting.* If you follow these keys you will begin to live your life by design versus default. You've absolutely got to decide today that you are the creative force for your life and that there's not one excuse out there that can stop you from truly living a life of deep meaning, passionate execution, and significant contribution. For you to truly make a major change in your life you are simply going to have take the time to just stop and think. Breakthroughs only happen when people stop and examine their underlying assumptions and realign internal dialogue that is deeply scripted in conscience with external actions. For the most part what I've experienced traveling the country is a profound misalignment between people's thoughts and actions and very little time to stop, reflect, and change to what they really want. Because of this cycle people only move in a direction they do not want to travel affected by people, environments, and other variables that leave them unsatisfied and unhappy. Today, that can change but you must first stop the business of your life, and reflect, and read on.

At the end of the day, it is important to understand this simple concept–*This Ain't No Practice Life.* Currently 41 percent of all Americans do not have a living will. Apparently they think they will live forever. Every day is crucial to living a life that matters. Time is vitally precious. No longer do you need to just think about the potential you have, you need to realize it. And the one thing you need to realize it is action. Talk is cheap in everyone's world. Now it is time to walk your talk and go realize the power of your life! As I write this book I'm reminded how much power words can have and how much they can impact others. I believe firmly that words can inspire and uplift because that's what good books have done for me. As we begin this journey I'm reminded of what William Faulkner said in his speech while accepting the Nobel Prize for Literature:

> *I believe that man will not merely endure: he will prevail. He is immortal, not because he alone among creatures has an inexhaustible voice, but because he has a soul, a spirit capable of compassion and sacrifice and endurance. The poet's, the writer's, duty is to write about these things. It is his privilege to help man endure by lifting his heart, by reminding him of the courage and honor and hope and pride and compassion and pity and sacrifice which has been the glory of*

his past. *The poet's voice need not merely be the record of man, it can be one of the props, the pillars to help him endure and prevail.*

My hope is that these writings will uplift and inspire you to work in the direction of your dreams and to begin the process of self-discovery in search of your passions. The journey will be well-worth the sacrifice and the payoff will be immeasurable. The ability to unlock the doors of fulfillment by having the right keys is very satisfying and will improve your quality of life in every dimension.

Enjoy the journey!

*Micheal*

# Part 1 - Finding your Voice

## Voice Means "Calling in Life"
*An Overview of* The Seven Keys to Significance

I think it is important to overview **the seven keys** in the order that the book is outlined. The keys are specifically positioned to go in sequential order and, if used properly, will unlock seven doors that will lead to more satisfaction and personal and professional fulfillment. I chose this terminology (keys and doors) because I believe that we choose to open doors in our lives at different times, but sometimes, for whatever reason we are either not ready or do not have the essential skills to go through those doors. Many times we simply do not have the right key to open the doors. The roadblock may be personal or professional; it may have to do with internal or external factors, levels of maturity, lack of experience, lack of wisdom, or simply a timing factor. How frustrating is it to need to get in a door to your house or car when you cannot find the right key? In our lives, not having the right keys is equally frustrating. This book will outline the doors that will be opened by using the right key and will unlock the potential to the infinite future.

# Overview of the Seven Keys to Significance

One Sunday I was sitting in the church in which I was raised listening to my preacher, Herb Alsup. He began to outline five important concepts that would help one get to heaven. I realized while I was listening that although life was messy and unpredictable, there were certain key principles that could help everyone improve. The process would require belief, faith, knowledge, self-awareness, imagination, and most importantly, action. As Herb spoke, I fervently took notes and visualized some similar principles that I could share with audiences. As I traveled, I began to see commonalities in what Herb said and what I was seeing all over the country. His words inspired me to come up with my own list of keys that would lead to personal fulfillment. I labeled them the *Seven Keys to Significance* and have shared them with individuals and organizations all over the country. If followed correctly, I believe these principles will steer you toward some level of success. It is up to you to decide what that level will be. They may appear obvious, but remember sometimes what is common sense is not always common practice. Think deeply about each key and begin to understand them at a deeper level as under each key in the book, there will be **seven** action items to help you unlock your potential and live a life of deep meaning and significant contribution.

## WAKE UP - Key No. 1 Unlocks the Door to Self-Awareness and Personal Responsibility

To get where you want to go, the first step is to confront the brutal facts about where you currently are. It is not possible to live in a fairy-tale world with fake trees and white elephants that I feel a good percentage of Americans live in. When it comes to waking up, you must first become highly proactive and take full responsibility for your lot in life. Your lot is yours and has been created by you and by the decisions and actions you have taken up until this point. You must begin to understand that we are where we are today because of all the choices we have made up until today. Accept and confront it and use the experiences that got you there as a stepping stone to the next level. Do a life inventory to see what is really going on with yourself. Check all your relationships, your vocation, your finances, your spirituality, your current limitations on your leadership style, your potential, and begin to get brutally honest with your success and failure in each one of those roles. You look right square in the mirror and make a decision that you will no longer live with mediocrity. Stephen Covey wrote in *The 8th Habit* (2004), "Everyone chooses one of two roads in life—the old and the young, the rich and the poor, men and women alike. One is the broad, well-traveled road to mediocrity, the other the road to greatness and meaning." He continues to say so powerfully, "The path to mediocrity straightjackets human potential. The path to greatness unleashes and realizes human potential. "Robert Frost so eloquently outlined in his poem *The Road Not Taken*, "Two roads diverged in a wood, and I, I took the one less traveled by. And that has made all the difference."

When you are ready to wake-up, you are ready to realize that life is about so much more than just making it through the day. Life is no longer about just surviving and barely keeping your head above water, it is about thriving, completing projects, helping others, connecting, acting on a mission, and living. Life is about working in a vocation and doing something significant with your time and your talents. To discover your true voice, you simply have to start the process by WAKING UP!

## DREAM UP - Key No. 2 Unlocks the Door to Imagination and Unlimited Potential

I do firmly believe in the Disney motto and a quote by Walt Disney, "If you can dream it, you can do it." The beauty of America is that you have the freedom and power to create a vision in your head (mental creation) and no one can stop you from fulfilling that vision (physical creation). The poor can become rich, the unsuccessful can become successful, the small can become the big, and the underdog can become the top dog if they only act. People gravitate toward big thinkers and the only way to truly tie yourself to a significant cause in your life is to think big thoughts and act on those thoughts. Remember, people do not regret what they do in life, they regret what they do not do. Between your stimulus and response is a space and in that space lies your freedom and ability to choose. If you live out of your imagination (infinite) instead of your memory (finite) you can begin with the end project in mind and work backward daily from that picture. Thomas Kuhn (1962) said in *The Structure of Scientific Revolutions*, "Every significant breakthrough that we have experienced in the world was first a break with an old thought pattern or paradigm into a new way of thinking." For you to live the life you want you have to break with old, outdated thought patterns into new ways of thinking. Simply put, if you want to experience success you have never experienced, you have to begin to think and act in ways that you have never thought before. There must be a break with the old into the new. You will hear me say frequently throughout this book, "You can't meet new challenges with old ways of thinking."

When you dream big you create a world from the mind's eye, a world full of opportunity and potential so vast and unbelievable that you will feel as if there is just not enough time for you to accomplish all you want to do in your life. You will approach every day with purpose and fervor and will see unlimited emotional power and endless possibilities. You will not be shackled by others perceptions or limited in your vocation. You will not accept no for an answer and will ultimately find a way to make your dreams a reality. Below is a list of paradigms that were simply limited. Just think if someone would have accepted the following premises and not challenged them:

1. "Nothing of importance happened today," written by King George III of England, on July 4, 1776.
2. "We don't like their sound. Groups of guitars are on the way out," Decca Records, rejecting the Beatles in 1962.
3. "There is no reason for any individual to have a computer in their home," Kenneth Olsen, president and founder of Digital Equipment Corporation, 1977.

Remember, you have the hammer and the nails to change it. Now go to work. When it comes to making money and dreaming remember this simple concept (that hit me like a ton of bricks one day while reading my horoscope): "Money does not grow on trees; it grows in the garden of your imagination. If you can dream it, you can make it." When you redefine what wealth means and replace financial wealth with happiness and fulfillment, you begin to dream big versus small and life is about a mission, not a paycheck. Many times if you chase being the best in your vocation, money will simply chase you. Start the process today of DREAMING UP!

# CLEAN UP - Key No.3 Unlocks the Door to Successful Projection and Inner Peace AND Removes the Toxic Energy from Your Life

This one is a no-brainer. If it walks like a duck, acts like a duck, and quacks like a duck, then most likely it is a duck. Same thing with winners. Eight out of ten times if she walks like a winner, talks like a winner, dresses like a winner, and acts like a winner, then she's a winner. To be successful dressing up simply won't do it, but getting rid of the toxins in your life such as energy drainers, clock eaters, and negative forces will be a strong step in the right direction. If you want to be first class then you have got to carry yourself and treat others first class. Every time you speak you are projecting and affirming to others how they should treat you. You have an opportunity daily to add value to others lives or detract value from their lives, and likewise them from you. When you begin to live from a paradigm of wholeness and goodness you operate from a moral compass that others can feel and see. You pull yourself out of activities that could detract from your reputation or perception and begin to associate with people that believe in your own worth and potential and lift you up versus tear you down. You operate from a perspective of abundance not scarcity, and see life as an adventure of the exchange of meaning and positive energy with others. You forgive those who have transgressed against you and come to the realization that we are all wayward travelers facing the same struggles in pursuit of the same thing: meaning and happiness.

One component of cleaning your life up is to be loyal to those who are absent by not participating in negative discussion about others behind their backs. "If you want to retain those who are present, be loyal to those who are absent" (Covey, 2004). Being loyal to those who are absent builds a strong brand of integrity to those both present and not present. People will secretly respect you more if you do not participant in the undermining of others when they are not present to defend themselves. This bad habit stems from insecurity and manifests itself from a scarcity mentality point of view. The abundance mentality teaches us that there is enough for everyone to have all they want, and we do not have to badmouth others in the process to get what we want. We make ourselves look inferior when we resort to trashing others. Secure people do not obtain confidence from making others look bad. They build up others or confront those they have challenges with and do it in a way that is respectful and balanced between courage and consideration (one strong sign of emotional maturity). Trust flows from trustworthiness and can only be gained by making deep deposits into the emotional bank accounts of others on a continual basis. Through this process of deep investment, one can truly transform the lives of others. Start today by cleaning out the trash in your life. Be loyal to those who are absent and be happy for the success of others. Petty jealousies only make you look weak and inferior and cast a glimpse into your real soul. Illuminate means to shine light on darkness. Illuminate your light on others every chance you get. It will come back around tenfold.

As you begin to clean your life up, you will begin to realize the benefits of continuing your education. I don't mean you have to go back to college, but you should constantly be engaged in educating the mind and the heart. From this continual process will flow opportunity and the ability to see situations from multiple dimensions actively expanding your circle of influence and building you into a commodity the world needs. You should be hungry to learn because this process of education builds both intellect quotient and emotional intelligence and continues to make you marketable to the world. As you grow your skills, you will discover that there will always be a place for your talents in the marketplace effectively making you a commodity in the workforce. This deep understanding alone unlocks the doors to opportunity and helps you to fully comprehend that you never have to go to a job you do not love–NEVER. You choose what you do for a living. Without education or training you may limit the opportunities you have, but with that training you will open more doors than you could ever handle. Each step of my educational journey I have only opened more doors and I know the single greatest driving force for that is continual learning. If you do not currently like your lot in life, go back to the education process until you become a solution to what the world needs and will pay you for. I will walk you through finding your voice in life which includes making major decisions about what you do for a living to meet the financial realities of your life. It all begins with CLEANING UP!

## LISTEN UP - Key No. 4 Unlocks the Door to Wisdom and Living a Conscience-Driven Life

Knowledge is all around us just knocking at our doors trying desperately to get in. I propose that we have been trained repeatedly in how to speak, write, and communicate, but have had less than two full weeks of training in how to listen. We have two ears, two eyes, and one mouth. With these we can listen and observe twice as much as we speak, but we don't always follow that adage. When you listen to others you are given a window into their souls. They are trying so badly to tell you how they feel, what they are interested in, what they stand for, what they are passionate about, and what they need from you. To be an effective person both personally and professionally, we have to listen up. Successful people observe and listen to everything that is around them, and they make a concerted effort to go and learn and listen to the great minds of their day. Not long ago, for the first time in my life, I was able to see and meet in person my greatest leadership mentor, Dr. Stephen Covey, author of *The 7 Habits of Highly Effective People* (1989). I listened with my head and my heart intently and searched for the deep meaning he was offering. I try to be a disciple to him so I can effectively influence others from the principles he teaches. If you want to be great at anything, open your heart and mind to the vast knowledge of those around you and practice empathic listening. Empathic listening is the practice of listening from another's frame of reference instead of your own. You are trying to feel where they are coming from and for a moment you trade perspectives with them and walk in their shoes. You listen from a dual perspective and act accordingly. If you want to be successful then listen up to the words being spoken. Listen from the intention of truly seeking to understand versus reply. Open and communicate with your heart and your soul. Seek first the benefit of others and listen to their stories and hear their songs. This will build compassion in you and allow you to become a light to others who may desperately need it. This will also build and educate your conscience which will serve you throughout your life.

Another facet of listening up is forming your own board of directors, a group of concerned and knowledgeable people who can help you through life's journey. This personal board of directors should meet with you a minimum of twice a year to offer guidance (both personally and professionally) to you as you navigate down the uncertain waters of life. This listening will offer wisdom. I saw not long ago a saying that said a good life was a series of good decisions. It then asked how do you make good decisions and said experience and wisdom. And how do you gain experience and wisdom? By making bad decisions. As you educate your conscience in the differences between right and wrong, you begin to be calm and quiet and simply listen to your internal voice. That voice, many times, will lead you exactly where you need to be and away from where you don't. Begin today by LISTENING UP!

## PAY UP - Key No. 5 Opens the Door to Consistent, Repetitive Work Toward a Destination and Uses Adversity to Accelerate Success

This key is not with money but with sacrifice. When it comes to success and significance the price must be paid and the process must be followed. There are no shortcuts to success. The law of the harvest certainly factors in here. Would you even ever dare to plant a garden and not water it, not offer it any sunlight, and expect it to be successful? Your life is exactly the same way. In your life you must "garden your garden" and tend to every aspect of it if you want to be successful. Be weary of the get rich quick scheme or the wealth without work approach. Anything worth having in life has to be earned. With growth sometimes comes pain but you can begin to see adversity as an accelerator to your progress not a stagnation to movement. If viewed from this perspective you approach the inevitable obstacles of life with grace and dignity, not as deal breakers to your future. The law of the harvest governs life which teaches us that we and nature are one as a "living system." Living systems are governed by natural laws or principles that are self-evident, timeless, and universal. When we neglect these principles we suffer consequences. Think about how nature operates on its own timetable that cannot be rushed. Success is the same way, a journey of exploration and inquiry into life. Gandhi proposed seven things would destroy us. If you take the time to study each very slowly, you can see how the law of the harvest is violated in each deadly sin:

1. Wealth without work
2. Pleasure without conscience
3. Knowledge without character
4. Commerce without morality
5. Science without humanity
6. Worship without sacrifice
7. Politics without principle

Each of these things can be obtained with false actions. The percentages are very small though for you to reach wealth without any work and the others six can be instrumental in your demise if acted on. The key lies in your ability to PAY the price and reap the benefit. For the actions in our life there are reactions from both the world and others. These reactions usually flow from predictable patterns. The natural consequence of you not being trustworthy is that others choose not to trust you. The natural consequence of you paying the price is that opportunity is afforded you. Once you understand this process you understand that everything is exactly as it should be at this moment in the world.

Many times in life you reach a certain level, similar to climbing a mountain. You believe that you are at the top when you reach a certain peak, but the reality of the situation is that when you get to that rise you are only at a level to see so much more than before. Paying the process will be exactly the same way. You will reach certain points where you will believe you have made some major progress only to be able to see so much more of life when you get there. I truly believe that with each year you live that you continue to expand and grow and with each day of learning you expand your horizons. Your mind and experiences will never digress to its earlier dimensions. Successful people who leave lasting impressions on society and in organizations are continuous learners who constantly pay the price of studying, reading, teaching, and growing. They seek new material like they seek air to breathe and see life as an upward spiral of continuous growth. With each circle they get better and better and "sharpen their saw" (Covey, 1989) knowing that by "sharpening their saw" they become a commodity in the world that others need. They truly add value to their lives and everyone they touch. The person that pays up is solutions oriented, not problem oriented, and obtains the skill set and tool set necessary to transcend any market place.

As you pay the price of significance understand that there will be rocks down life's gravel road. It is not what happens to us that hurts us, it is ultimately our response to what happens that does. Understand that there are three options offered by Collins (2001) in *Good to Great* in a study by the Center for Victimization. This study focused on individuals who suffered major adversity that ranged from cancer patients to people involved in serious automobile accidents. The three responses included people who were permanently disabled by the event (they did not recover), those who just got their lives back to normal, and those who used the event as a defining moment to their future success. Think about how you handle adversity. If you are going to pay up, you understand that heartache will certainly be some of the cost of doing business. Use that as a way to build character in your life and as a well spring of inspiration for yourself and others.

Part of paying up is also the process of growing your influence. This process is one of constantly working at the outside edge of your circle of influence by taking initiative and showing others that you are a catalyst for positive change and growth. As you make and keep your commitments to others you see yourself growing in both influence and responsibilities in the workplace and in the community as others begin to respect you in ways that only affirms the worth and potential in you. This new influence taps into your conscience's need to connect to something larger than yourself. This process is very liberating to the soul and solidifies yourself in the world as you begin to make positive improvements to the world and with people with whom you interact.

# BUILD UP - Key No. 6 Unlocks the Door of Synergy, Affirmation in Others, and Unlimited Potential in the Power of a Team

Zig Ziglar said, "If you help enough people get what they want in life, you'll get what you want." I totally agree. As I get older I have begun to get so much satisfaction from building others up. When you build others up you affirm the self-worth and potential in them so much that they truly begin to illuminate it in themselves. You should seek every opportunity you can to affirm the worth and potential in others. As you begin to see the good in others they will begin, like a mirror, to reflect the good in you as well. **The key many times to success is to the one.** Build relationships one at a time in your personal and professional lives. Invest the time and the energy to ignite others' fires and watch and see how it manifests in your life. When you reach a certain point on the maturity continuum, you begin to understand and fully realize that you have the ability to have tremendous influence in the world. I mentioned my encounter with Dr. Stephen Covey earlier. He flattered and built me up by signing a copy of his book and writing that I was a trim-tab, a metaphor for one who uses his power of influence to effectively change the lives of many. A trim-tab on a boat or ship is the small rudder that turns the big rudder that turns the entire ship. These people can move themselves and their team or departments in such a way that it positively affects the entire organization. A trim-tab exercises high levels of initiative within his or her circle of influence until that circle expands exponentially and disciples are created. We could all be trim-tabs in any situation because leadership is a choice.

Successful people look out the window to give credit to others when things go well and look in the mirror to accept blame when things go wrong (Collins, 2001). When you build others up, you connect your heart and spirit with the need to leave a legacy in your life and that can only be done by thinking beyond yourself. Every significant contribution in the world was done by and with others. The reality of the situation is that we live in an interdependent society and the only way the world will ever survive is through this concept. We must build others up and not resort to scarcity mentality thinking where we constantly tear others down and get caught up in confessing the sins of others. Look for golden opportunities to have crucial conversations that connect to others that will put money in their emotional bank account. Seek daily to build as many people as you can up and watch how they return that kindness and courtesy to you. "Be a light, not a judge, be a model, not a critic" (Covey, 2004). Start today by BUILDING UP all those you come in contact with. You can do this by giving a gift of a compliment to all you touch along the journey!

## ACT UP - Key No. 7 Unlocks the Door to Execution and Completion

Og Mandino (1968) said in *The Greatest Salesman in the World*, "My goals are worthless, my plans are impossible, and none will be of any value unless followed by action." Each of the first six keys to success will take you no where unless you have the self-discipline to act on them. The execution gap across this country is mind boggling. So many people just think and talk but never connect the dots to the most important phase of living a meaningful life around action and execution. Let me pose this question to you. If you knew that you only had six months to live would you be so hesitant to act on your dreams? Would you be hesitant to build others up? Would you be so consumed with working every second of every day? Would you get so irate about the minute things in your life? Would you take for granted those important souls who have come into your life for a reason? My guess is no. My personal mission statement starts with four words—Passion, Patience, Persistence, and Perseverance—because I believe you need these four attributes to live a life of deep meaning and significant contribution. At the bottom of that mission statement I added the most powerful mission statement of all—live like you were dying. If you were to live like you were dying, you would most certainly ACT. You would reconcile every situation in your life that was heavy on your heart. You would forgive every person that has transgressed against you. You would work each day with passion and meaning and would look for golden teachable moments to make a difference in the lives of others. You would see time for exactly what it is, the most precious commodity you have. You would not be so caught up in material things, the petty arguments, the insecurities, the jealousies, and the success of others. You would truly operate within your circle of influence to use your time and talents wisely. You would live life to the fullest. You know the best advice I could give you today is

*"Go live like you were dying!"*

# The Process of Unlocking the Doors— The Belief and Action Model

To use the *Seven Keys to Significance* to unlock the doors to your potential there is a sequential process to follow as illustrated in figure 1. This model was developed through a discussion with a friend and fellow businessman and consultant Tony Woodall. He and I collaborated on its contents on the way to a speaking assignment in Bristol, Tenn. The model begins with believing that it is possible for you to have anything that you want in life. From this belief stems a vision or seeing of what you want. This seeing has not manifested yet but is the seed of the fruit you are going to produce. This is the mental creation, or seeing the world through the mind's eye. From the mental creation, action must be attached to see results. Unfortunately people breakdown either in the belief stage or in the action stage which prohibits them from ever fully realizing their potential. In an effort to achieve results you really need to focus growing yourself in four key areas: knowledge (for the mind), skills (for the body), desire (for the heart), and belief (for the spirit). Any fragmentation of these four dimensions will result in not realizing your potential and will result in stifled growth and stagnation toward bringing your vision to manifestation.

As Tony notes, there are two types of manifestation that takes place in our lives. The first is intentional manifestation where we intentionally co-create something happening in life. We believe it can happen, we visualize it, we act on our vision, and we reflect on what we accomplished. This book operates primarily from that paradigm. The second form of manifestation is unintentional, or where things emerge in your life as a result of connection to your source and conscience. This is an interesting phenomenon and one that we will explore in another book. Once you go through the first three parts of creating results in your life it is vitally important to STOP and reflect on those results to see what worked and what needs to be changed to build future capacity. This reflection challenges you to see how your actions affected both you and others and encourages you to move to an age of wisdom. Tony's model of manifestation is similar centered on a three-step process in the personal aspect: knowing, dreaming, and being. From the professional perspective he postulates the process to be knowledge, imagination, and manifestation. For the purposes of this book we will use the following model titled *The Belief and Action Model.*

## Figure 1. The Belief and Action Model

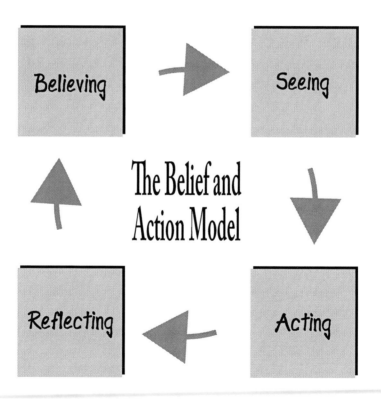

*Believing, Seeing, Acting, Reflecting*

Now that you have an overview of the seven keys, it is important to learn them at a deeper level. "To know and not to do is really not to know" (Covey, 2004). The *Belief and Action Model* will be of no value to you unless you truly practice its contents with the skill set and knowledge base to actively change areas of your life and sustain that change. Each key has seven important ways to manifest improvement in your life followed by seven action items in the summaries. If practiced these seven keys will open the doors necessary to improve your capacity to live, to love, to learn, and to leave a legacy.

# Chapter 1 - Wake Up

## Key No.1 Unlocks the Door to Self-Awareness and Responsibility

*Seven Facts to Confront*

# 1. Understand the Value of Time and Your Life

I think every person should wake up in the morning with a purpose and a reason for living. To do this you must first come to a very strong realization. Your time is THE most precious commodity you will ever have. How you choose to spend and invest your time determines your quality of life. In this section I want to open your eyes to how most people spend theirs. The average person spends 23 years of his/her life sleeping, 9 ½ years in the car, 6 years eating, 1-5 years participating in religious activity, 6 months to a year waiting at red lights, 140 days over a lifespan making and unmaking the bed, between 15-20 years in some form of education, and here's the kicker, between 35-50 years working. Now how important is your time? Even though 70% of all people do not like their jobs, the average person spends 12-14 hours per day working just to get through what's on her plate (let alone doing anything significant or important), and 88% say it is hard to balance personal and professional lives. The average person receives six voice mail messages per day and sits in 1.6 meetings that 85% say are unimportant and 88% say had absolutely nothing to do with the mission of the organization. Now how important is your time? My point is this: there is no such thing as *time management*. Can you speed up, slow down, or stop time?

At many of the seminars I teach across the country people want to know how they can better manage their time and the point is that you can't. You don't manage time. You spend it with people you care about, you invest it in things and people you deem worthy, or you flat out waste it. It is that simple. The key to managing your time is to decide what is most important to you (quality of life) and place those things, those people, and those activities into your time allotment. On many occasions the people I work with allow things, agendas, and work schedules to dominate their lives and then take the role of victim when that could not be further from the truth. You control your life and you certainly control how you invest your time. Don't ever let anyone else tell you any differently.

Think about this. If I were to give you $86,400 this morning and told you that at 12:00 midnight you lost any you didn't use and it did not carry over until the next day, what would you do with that money? Typical answers I get at seminars are spend it, invest it, or waste it. Those are all good answers. We all know people that spend the money they have on people they love. We all know that some people waste the money they have. If you do not believe that, then study the number of people who go bankrupt after winning the lottery. We also know people that might invest the money to build future capacity. The key here is this: we all have something far more precious than $86,400 per day although that's hard to believe. We have 86,400 seconds per day. My guess is that you still fall into one of those three categories: you are spending it with people you love or in causes you deem worthy, investing it with people you care about through wisdom and teaching, or you are flat out wasting it. Smart people try to spend and invest their 168 hours per week in activities and people that make them happy and fulfilled. It is also vitally important to have a nice balance between personal and professional life. If you get all of your satisfaction off the job or on the job then it is time to evaluate the quality of things you are placing your time in other areas.

Now that you have a better understanding of how people spend their time, you need to understand that everyday you make four bets with yours. Mark LeBlanc, owner of *Small Business Success*, and the biggest person who influenced me to write my first book says that, "Everyday you make four bets: your time, energy, money, and creativity." I agree. What goes into your time in those four areas will ultimately come out on the other end. Be a poor planner and steward of that time and you will most likely one day regret you didn't do something meaningful with yours.

There are two simple models you can use when it comes to your life. Organize, act, and evaluate or continue, stop, and start. These are simple concepts that pay enormous dividends. Living effectively is a continual process of adjustments based on seeing the need and filling the need and something you must do daily. Always remember, "Where there's no gardener, there's no garden." Think about how much you are tending to your garden. As I discuss the importance of planning the use of your time it is vitally important to know and connect to your mission in life and to do that you need a mission statement or defining statement. I'll discuss this later under the second key of fulfillment, *Dream Up*. As you begin to grow yourself in the four key areas—knowledge, skills, desire, and belief—you build capacity to accept full responsibility for your life and your actions around how you spend your time. Remember, quality of life begins with how you choose to spend or invest your time. Most of the successful people I know accept full responsibility for their lives and do not blame the past, the environment, or others for how they choose to live.

# 2. Become Responsible for Your LIFE— The Habit of Proactivity

At the heart of the term proactivity is accepting FULL responsibility for your lot in life. It means that you have the power to choose your response to any situation you encounter in life, that you can take the initiative to change the way you see any situation instantaneously, and that although you may predisposed to certain genetic, psychological, or physiological factors; you are not determined by them. My point is simple; YOU ALWAYS HAVE A CHOICE! The outcome of recognizing this is that if you want to change anything in your life, you can. As you begin to practice mindfulness and grow your self-awareness you hide from nothing and you accept both positive and negative thoughts and circumstances in your life. You bring an awareness of what is actually going on. Through self-awareness (the ability to reflect on your life as you live it), imagination (the ability to create a better world in your head), independent will (the ability to act on what you want to change), and conscience (a sense of right and wrong), you can change. Bad habits are like the strong pull of gravity pulling you right back where you don't need to be. To break these bad habits you will have to acknowledge them first and accept the truth as it is. You will not be able to meet new challenges or garner new successes with old ways of thinking on old habits. Remember, to make a new contribution to this world and to your life, you must create a whole new preparation.

As you begin to understand this powerful concept, you move away from becoming the opposite of proactive, which is reactive. Reactive people blame others for their lots in life, make excuses when they don't get the results they want, and spend their lives disempowering themselves and allowing the weaknesses of others to control them. Reactive people become negative the first time something goes wrong and very rarely want to accept responsibility for anything, unless it is successful.

Author Victor Frankl (1997) who wrote *Man's Search for Meaning* noted while in a Nazi prison camp being severely mistreated that no one could take away what he called his "Last Human Freedom" which was the power to choose his response to virtually any situation in life. Between stimulus and response (see diagram) is a space and in that space lies our ability to choose.

**Figure 2**

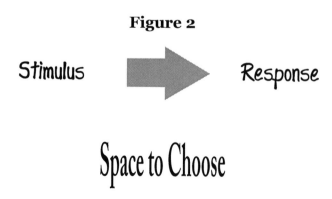

To live a life of deep meaning and significant contribution of service to others we must develop the capacity or self-discipline to ACT within that space. The only lasting form of discipline is self-discipline but that discipline must be cultivated by winning the private victory over one's moods or feelings. The term sacrifice means to subordinate what one wants now for what one wants later. It is only after we accept full responsibility for our actions and completely understand that we have a choice in all situations that we become responsible for our lives and make the shift from reactive to proactive.

When you take this responsibility you will gain a deep level of freedom. It will be emancipating and liberating to take back control of your thoughts, your beliefs, your vision, and your actions. This freedom will open the door to the self-imposed prisons of blaming, criticizing, contending, comparing, and allowing others thoughts, actions, or words to control your life. You will truly be set free.

# 3. Confront the Brutal Facts of Your Life— Without Losing Faith That You Can Get Where You Are Going

One of the hardest things we will ever have to do is to confront the brutal facts of our lives while at the same time never losing faith that we will reach where we are going through consistent, repetitive, deliberate action. In the end, the process will be of far greater value than the product, and we must always value the journey along the way. It is there where the most memories and impact of others will take place. The easy thing to do in life is to live in a dreamworld and not confront the difficulties, the insecurities, the shortcomings, and the failures. However, if viewed properly, these are essential stepping stones to success.

Confronting the brutal facts means not living a lie and owning and accepting who you are, what you have done no matter how it affects how others perceive you, recognizing mistakes and transgressions against others, and moving to a place of peace and harmony. We must all realize that we are where we are today because of all the decisions we made up until today. As we become vulnerable and understand that we all have challenges in our lives, we understand that we do not have to conceal those vulnerabilities but only embrace them and work to improve them.

This also means we have to create relationships with others, both personally and professionally, where the truth is heard and facts are given. To many times we sugarcoat to our friends and co-workers what is actually happening and that leaves them with skewed facts with which to work and inaccurate paradigms for reflection. As we become vulnerable and confront the facts we must also NEVER lose faith that we will move forward. In *Key No. 5–Pay Up* I will discuss using adversity to accelerate progress in your life but you can only do this if you accept the situation as it is (not filtered), take responsibility for the situation, and work with a focus, faith, and passion to change the situation. Dr. Phil often says, "We cannot change what we won't acknowledge." This is the step of acknowledgement that is critical to turning the wheels of change. Confront where you are today and have unwavering faith that you will get where you are going. This vision, seeing the world through the mind's eye, coupled with discipline will help you use the facts to create the world you want, versus being a victim of the one you are currently occupying.

# 4. Complete an Inventory of Your Life— Get real!

"The history of free man is never written by chance but by choice—their choice."

*Dwight D. Eisenhower*

I have the ultimate questions for you, and I want you to look right in the mirror and not out the window for the answer. I want you to get really serious, confront the brutal facts, and increase your self-awareness so that you can give yourself an honest answer to these questions. The most important conversations in your life will be the ones you have with yourself. Isn't it about time to start having the life you really want? Isn't it time to have the career you want, drive the car you want, be in a relationship with the person you want, associate with the friends you like, go to church where you want, get involved with the project you want, volunteer like you want, lose the weight you want, build the house you want, and live the way you want. Folks, it is past time. No longer should you use the excuses of fear of failure, laziness, insecurity, fear of embarrassment, lack of self-discipline, activity trap of life, or whatever you want to place between you knowing what type of life you want to have and you actually creating it. It is time to understand, *This Ain't No Practice Life*. Consider this quote:

"I am no longer a young man filled with energy and vitality. I'm given to meditation and prayer. I would enjoy sitting in a rocker, swallowing prescriptions, listening to soft music, and contemplating the things of the universe. But such activity offers no challenge and makes no contribution. I wish to be up and doing. I wish to face each day with resolution and purpose. I wish to use every waking hour to give encouragement, to bless those whose burdens are heavy, to build faith and strength of testimony. It is the presence of wonderful people which stimulates the adrenaline. It is the look of love in their eyes which gives me energy."

*Gordon B. Hinckley, Age Ninety-Two*

What do you wish to be doing today? In high school one of my toughest and most challenging teachers, Barbara Parker, asked us to do an exercise where we basically wrote out the life we would like to have. At the time we didn't fully understand the exercise but in its essence it now carries tremendous power. I wrote all the things I wanted to do with my life as if I actually did write that program. After grading the paper she returned it to us with a very strong question. In bright red ink on the back it said, "Then why aren't you doing it?" It wasn't until years later that I fully appreciated that question and believe enough in it to share it with you. If you were to write down the life you really wanted to live including the career you wanted to have, the house you wanted to live in, the relationship you wanted to be in, the community member everyone appreciated, the family member you aspired to be, the friend you would like to have, the true person you wanted to be, the car you wanted to drive, the vacation you'd like to be on and on and on and on, what would those things say? My question to you is why aren't you doing all of those things with your life? You do have control over it, don't you? We get one ride on this merry go round and your choices are simple: live a life of design or a life of default. My advice to you is to choose wisely.

By taking an inventory right now of your life and consistently reflecting on how you are choosing to spend your time you can make decisions based on what is most important versus simply what is urgent at the time. If you are not careful, urgency and activity traps of life will drive all your time leaving you unhappy and unfulfilled. An effective persons wakes up, consistently studies where he spends his/her time, and makes the necessary adjustments to live life by design (you create it) versus default (other people or circumstances creates it).

Dr. Phil McGraw became increasingly popular with millions of people across the world when he used the term "get real" about your life several years ago. I believe that we all at times fall into predictable categories that I've outlined in my "five levels of life." You can move up the ladder to where you are a "Level 5 Doer and Achiever." Most people have the latent and undeveloped potential to move up the food chain, they just have to have the initiative and educated conscience to do so. Real significance is harnessed at the fifth level so your goal should be to continuously move up the ladder of success.

To complete an inventory of your life you must fully embrace where you are. Several years ago, when writing my first book, *Changing Lives through Coaching*, I created a maturity continuum that offered a picture of where you could be today. If you locate yourself on this continuum and do not like where you are, do not worry, we can always change it. Here are five levels of people:

**Category 1 (Reactors)** - You spend your life responding (or reacting) to whatever life throws at you. You wake up in the morning with little or no direction and float through the galaxy dodging bullets and just trying to "survive." If you are in this category, leading yourself or other people will be very difficult. After all, how can you inspire others when you can't inspire yourself? The reactors typically complain about their lots in life and blame a host of others for their failures. They live their lives as a function of other people's weaknesses or circumstances which they believe they have little control over. They're the opposite of proactive which at its core means to take full responsibility for the success or failure of your life. The reactor blames other people or the environment for their failure. It is never their fault. I bet you know or work with a whole host of those! You must focus solely on your circle of influence to change the things in your life for which you are reactive about. Reactors very rarely get ahead in life, but usually waste the precious time they've been given. If you are in this category we need to light your fire immediately and help you to understand the importance of connecting to an important mission and being forward looking. Don't let your past hold your future hostage. The unfortunate part of most reactors is that they have developed a functional blindness to their own defects. They could never see themselves as reactive so that very thought limits their awareness and ability to act. As we grow our knowledge, we also grow our ignorance. I know it is a paradox but really intelligent people understand, "The more you know, the more you don't know." Until we become humble and teachable we can never fully grow and get better. This self-awareness will either propel our growth or limit our progress.

**Category 2 (Strugglers)** - You know what you want to do with your life, but you do not know how to get it. You have not paid the real price for success or invested in the education or training necessary to thrive in today's global market place. You have not gardened your garden and know it deep down. You may have the vision but lack the discipline and passion to execute the plan to achieve success. Because of this reactive planning you become frustrated and intimidated and think success is out there, but only for the lucky and the strong, and you don't perceive yourself to be in either of those two categories. Remember this: *ALL* the successful people in the world started somewhere and many of them from less than glamorous situations. If you don't believe me just watch the hundreds of episodes of any biographical show that outlines a star's rise from virtually nothing. Decide today that you are going to be one of those people and get started. The struggling category means you are being paralyzed because you have limiting perceptions. Change the picture and believe in yourself because others won't until you do. If you are in this category the key word is *belief*. You see, confidence comes only from the memory of success and success can only be achieved by consistent, repetitive practice. If you want to move out of the struggling phase, act, over and over again until you feel confident that you can do it. If you want to stay right where you are, try one time, and when it does not work become frustrated and intimidated. This guarantees stagnation and complacency. Unfortunately some people live in complacent worlds and only complain about them.

**Category 3 (Thinkers)** - You know what you want, you know how to get it but you are caught in an activity trap, the business of life, and you just can't get started on those hopes and dreams. These are the *someday* people. Next year I'll improve or be the person that I envision. I just can't right now because I am so busy. There are certainly no guarantees for tomorrow and the last time I checked, *today* is the most important day of your life. Leadership expert John C. Maxwell says, "Yesterday's a cancelled check; tomorrow's a promissory note, so today is the only day that really matters." The first step on the path to greatness is to overcome inertia. You have all the tools so go for it. My motto is, "There is only one way in life to profit, and that is by taking a risk." The only real risk is riskless living. Stick your neck out and remember, you will miss 100 percent of the shots you do not take and miss 100 percent of the dreams you do not pursue. The next time you have a great idea that you are passionate about write it down and then act on it. Two thousand people might tell you it is absurd but if my memory serves me correctly that's how many times Thomas Edison tried to invent the light bulb before it worked. Consider it a 2,000-step process. The next step on the maturity level that follows creating a vision is creating the discipline and passion and having a properly educated conscience to execute that vision. If you are a thinker, we're headed in the right direction but the equation is simply fragmented and incomplete until you act. You have got to connect more of the dots to have a happy ending.

**Category 4 (Quick fixers/Short-term thinker)** - You know what you want, you know how to get it, and you go out into the real world to try it but you fail for reasons in and out of your control. As a result you become cynical and pessimistic about the process and just stay right where you are. Your failure reaffirms that you knew you could not attain your goal and your shortcoming is only proof of your non-existence and shallow thinking. Folks, the going rate for any worthwhile win is 10 setbacks. The tenth try might be the trick and all the others could be unanswered prayers. Only time will tell, but you are sure to fail if you feel sorry for yourself or think that people always get it right the first time. I have been rejected for several jobs and all of the rejections have turned out to be blessings in disguise. I'm sure you have your own list too of what seemed to be a disaster at the time, only later to find out that what happened was one of the best things that ever happened to you. If you do fail a number of times, get in line with the millions of people that do so every day. Learn from it and move on to the next available opportunity. The right fit will certainly come along sooner rather than later if you focus on your circle of influence and keep improving your skills. Harvey Mackay's (2004) book *We Got Fired!: . . . And It's the Best Thing That Ever Happened to Us* outlines several successful people who were fired. When adversity hits ask one simple question, "What is this trying to teach me?" I'll outline ways later in the book to actually use adversity to accelerate progress in your life versus allowing it to become debilitating and paralyzing.

**Category 5 (Doers and Achievers)** - You are the movers and shakers of the world. The average person can't keep up with you because the word average doesn't fit into your language system. You are proactive, self-disciplined, have enormous amounts of emotional intelligence, have found your voice in life, and are on your way to living a life of deep meaning and significant contribution. Smart people will do one thing, harness your potential and let you go. They will get out of your way and let you work. A smart leader would hire as many of these people as possible because they will build enduring organizations and make a lasting impact on others. You will be disappointed occasionally to find out that some of the world just does not get you and cannot figure out why you just will not be stagnant and quit trying to improve everything. The truth is that most of those people want to be like you and cannot stand that you are making things happen. Expect a lot of resistance from many of the people you come in contact with because they are absolutely scared to death of change and may not be as intrinsically motivated as you are. Do not let them stop you or remotely slow you down just ask them quietly to get out of your way. You keep on keeping on, fight the good fight everyday, and know that you are doing something that matters and are proceeding in an upward spiral of improvement towards your hopes and dreams. Category 5 people are the ones that make a significant difference in the lives of others. They leave unwavering legacies in organizations that will never be forgotten and truly understand the difference between transformation and transaction.

# 5. Win the Private Victory of Your Life

The toughest battles you will ever fight will be the internal struggles you have between the what you are doing, and what you should be doing. Some refer to this as creative tension—the gap between your current reality and the future reality you wish to create. Conscience, if educated properly, drives our decision making, if we only would listen to it more often. I will discuss the importance of listening to your small, still voice from within later in *Key No. 4—Listen Up.*

As you begin to flex your emotional muscles and to build the capacity to make and keep commitments to yourself, you will then grow your capacity to meet the needs of others. Part of the process of finding your own voice is possessing the ability to make and keep commitments and promises to yourself. Doing this breaks down old habits of lack of execution and builds new internal muscles that help you meet the challenges of a permanent whitewater society. The emotional tension and anxiety of not translating thoughts into action will evaporate, and you will view the creative tension between current reality and hopeful reality as energy that will promote positive change.

When you lift weights you experience a certain pain. That pain is prompted by the breaking down of muscle fibers which then rebuild themselves and become even stronger after the workout. You must first meet the challenge, go beyond past limitations, and then work to go into new arenas of success. This process is the equivalent of building the emotional strength to build the capacity necessary to meet whatever comes your way. Only when you have paid the price to the personal victory will you be able to have the public victory. If your life is flawed with internal conflict and your own inability to make and keep promises to yourself first, you will never be able to lead others or serve in productive ways because your friends and colleagues will detect this duplicity from your actions and your trustworthiness will be negated.

# 6. Find Your Unique Voice

Finding your unique voice in life will be one of the most important journeys you will ever take. Detecting this voice (calling in life) will begin the process of unleashing the enormous talent and potential inside of you and will awaken the passion to move to the next level in your life where you can then begin to inspire others. It is the equivalent of developing your gift in life and giving that gift away to as many people as you can. As I speak on this across the country I am amazed at how many people have never begun the process of discovering their voices and therefore have lived in self-imposed prisons of jobs as occupations versus contributing in careers as vocations. As we reflect on how we invest our time we begin to understand that a quality life revolves around a holistic approach that taps into our four birth gifts for which we are stewards: body, mind, heart, and spirit. Follow the needs of each of these endowments and see where you are lacking:

1. The body needs to live and meet the economic realities of the world. This is PQ or physical intelligence.
2. The mind needs to learn, grow, and expand. This is IQ or intellect quotient.
3. The heart needs to love something or somebody and to be loved. This is EQ or emotional intelligence.
4. The spirit needs to connect to something larger, to be a part of something meaningful, to contribute. It also has a need to connect to conscience and act in thoughtful ways to human kind. This is SQ or spiritual intelligence.

In essence what this model represents is a four-dimensional paradigm to finding your voice in life. To break that down would mean that most people have a deep need:

1. To live (body)
2. To learn (mind)
3. To love (heart)
4. To leave a legacy (spirit)

As we explore this "whole-person" theory introduced by my favorite author, Stephen Covey, we begin the process of finding our unique voices by tapping into body, mind, heart, and spirit. As we find that voice here are some specific questions to ask:

1. What are you deeply passionate about?
2. What could you be the best in the world at?
3. What drives your economic engine?

## Simple Ways to Detect Your Voice
### *The Process Is Just as Important as the Product!*

As we travel through life we begin to get excited about things even to the point that we become obsessed with them. They light our fire, they give us cause to wake up for in the morning, we deem them worthy of our time, and we give our whole self to being good at them. That is our passion and that is where we need to be investing our time. I am asked all of the time, "How do I figure out what I am passionate about?" or "How do I know if my passions are evolving?" I think both questions are perfectly legitimate. Let me give you a couple of simple ways to find and detect your passion because I truly believe when we are deciding how to spend our time, passion has to be involved. Be sure you fully understand, it is my belief that passion is not some quick-fix buzz word that is overused (contrary to some speaker's words). It may be underdone and underdeveloped, but people need to be talking about passion all the time because it is the gas that drives your engine. Without it, life is dull and mundane. We need passion in our jobs, in our relationships, in our hobbies, and in virtually everything we do. If you are trying to detect your passion ask yourself these questions:

1. What would I drive all night through two states to talk to five people for free?
2. What would I work 40 hours a week for free if I knew it would lead to peace of mind, happiness, financial freedom, and fulfillment in the long run?
3. What do I get excited about when I talk about it?
4. What could I spend hours researching?
5. What do I truly love at my core?

When you begin to answer these questions, you will begin the process of finding your passion. It is entirely feasible that your passion will evolve over the years. I began as just a basketball coach trying to win games and have evolved into a person who wants to influence millions of people. My passion has evolved from just coaching to developing leaders and influencing people to do something significant with their lives. Find your passion, do it for a living, and you will never work another day the rest of your life. Once you answer those questions you are on your way to choosing a vocation that will bring significance to your life.

## Understanding the Difference between Occupation and Vocation
### *The Difference between a Pay Check and a Significant Life*

In this section, I felt that it was vitally important to mention the difference between occupation and vocation as the legacy our lives are tied to will most likely be made during our careers. When one goes to choose a craft it is vitally important to create that synergy between passion, talent, needs of the world, and conscience. Remember, the body has a need to live, the mind has a need to learn, the heart has a need to love and be passionately involved with a worthy cause, and the spirit has a need to leave a legacy in life. If any one of these areas is neglected then an imbalance will occur resulting in unhappiness and lack of fulfillment. To find your voice (using the questions on the preceding page), you can choose to be involved with a vocation, stemming from a Latin word meaning "voice" or "calling" in life which offers you the opportunity to become a disciple of a cause or project you think is worthy of your time. Occupation simply means that which occupies your time for which you receive a paycheck. Now which would you really like to go to? An occupation or a vocation? Part of practicing the concepts in this book challenge you to look inward and explore the latent and undeveloped gifts you have to offer, find those gifts, and give those gifts away during your transactions with others. When your work, play, and love all intersect then you've got passion and that's an irresistible belief for motive and action. Now is the time to decide what you want your vocation to be and quit just making it through the day by going to that occupation. Remember, your voice is your gift in life and that gift is so valuable that it must be risked and given to others. By hoarding your talent you are ensuring that it will never be used, and there is no tragedy as strong as the unopened gift. As you study the following diagram, give serious thought to these five questions. I believe strongly that they hold the key to unlocking your future significance:

1. What are the latent talents that I have been given?
2. What are the needs in the world that people will pay me to fulfill?
3. What can I be a part of that taps into my conscience, my need for meaning, and my desire to connect to something larger than myself?
4. What am I deeply passionate about?
5. What drives my economic engine? How much money do I need to make to meet the realities of my world?

**Figure 3**
**Finding Your Unique Voice at the**
**Intersection of the Five Circles**

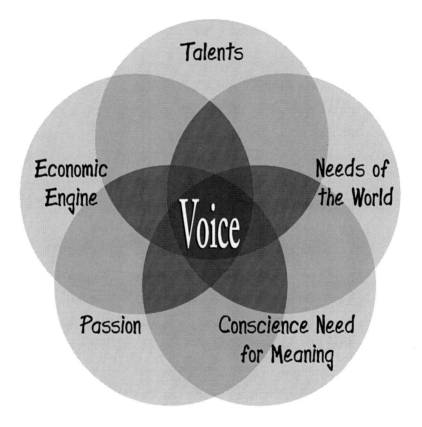

I truly believe as you go through this model that its contents will be validated by helping you find your voice at the nexus or intersection of these five circles. Not long ago, I took this test myself while flying back from a speaking engagement. There were certain areas I needed to refine but for the most part I figured out that I had found my voice in life. This gave me tremendous satisfaction both personally and professionally to know that I was involved in projects in life that paid me fairly (body), treated me kindly (heart), used me creatively (mind), and tapped into my conscience for meaning (spirit). Now that you know how to detect your voice it is time to begin the process of intentional manifestation in your life.

# 7. Understand The Best Way to Predict the Future of Your Life Is to Create It

The final key to opening the door to responsibility and self-awareness in your life is to understand that the best way to predict your future is to create it. By building your capacity through self-discipline, becoming proactive versus reactive, by taking an inventory of your life, and by finding and detecting your unique voice in life you can then become the creative force for your life. Your fire will be lit by your passions and you fully understand that we only get one life and what we do with that life solely rests within our circle of influence and control.

Once we grasp this powerful concept, we begin to work at the outside edge of that initiative to grow our influence and begin to move in a powerful direction in an upward spiral of improvement and growth at an unstoppable pace. We are internally driven to succeed, no matter what. We then take full responsibility for our lives and realize that if we want to do better for ourselves then we must create that life. From this perspective we write the book of our life and have the power and capacity to live from that book.

One of the most difficult challenges we will face will be the ability to act in a way that we have predetermined around our core value system in times of stress or pressure. I wrote in my second book, *The Inspirational Leader*, that being the person at the end of the day that we set out to be in the beginning is an enormous character builder. When we create synergy between our walk and our talk, we begin to cultivate the integrity in our lives which represents wholeness and goodness.

The most difficult aspect of leading will be telling yourself you want to lead one way daily only to have the many stimuli of environmental conditions to push out of being that person. The same principle applies to waking up and fully grasping the concept that you are in charge of your actions. No other person can make you feel a certain way, can facilitate a bad mood, can change your mind, can treat you poorly, or can decide your success or failure in this world without your consent. Once you can operate from this paradigm, you can drive your own boat. I use the boat analogy because as I write this I'm cruising through the Pacific Ocean on a cruise to Alaska. If you could only see what I see, you would want to wake up and take full responsibility for your life because you would understand the immense benefits of taking control of your own destiny.

There are a few reasons why we do not attempt to create our future. They are:

1. Fear of failure—stagnates growth
2. Not enough faith in the outcome—creates hopelessness
3. Fear of the work involved—causes boredom and stagnation
4. Afraid of the journey—causes life to become dull and mundane
5. Lack of education—creates atrophy in the brain
6. Limited beliefs—most likely instilled during primitive years
7. Reactive to the negative pull of the surrounding environment

Working with people in all parts of the world, I have used the body, mind, heart, and spirit model to accurately diagnose and prescribe most of the ills people face both personally and in the workplace. Just take a moment to reflect on what happens when

- you are not paid fairly to meet the economic realities of the world. Or you do not take care of your physical body and you cannot perform at optimum levels. *(Body)*

- you are not used creatively, you don't challenge your mind, you don't grow, and you allow yourself to fall victim to atrophy and stagnation. *(Mind)*

- you are not treated kindly, you do not project love to others, and you are not passionate about the causes you involve yourself with. *(Heart)*

- you do not believe in the mission of what you are doing, you are dispirited by events, or you have lost faith in the messenger or the message. *(Spirit)*

The clear result of these violations manifests in these ways:

- You seek additional jobs—you moonlight, or you become lethargic and stagnate which leaves you empty and unfulfilled. *(Body)*

- You daydream, you become dull, you become unmarketable, or you check in and pick up a paycheck but do not commit your true intellect. *(Mind)*

- You withdrawal to protect yourself, you become disengaged, you lose your passion, or you just quit altogether. *(Heart)*

- You become dispirited, lost, broken, and you lose all faith in the mission of what you are doing. *(Spirit)*

As you can see violating any of these four dimensions of the "whole person" will result in profound misalignment of conscience. This disconnect will eat away at your soul. This places an enormous emphasis on finding your voice in life and creating balance in all dimensions so you are living a life that really matters to you and your associates. To manifest these actions, begin by practicing the seven key habits and watch your own credibility with yourself grow and expand exponentially.

# Chapter 1 Summary— Seven Action Items to Manifest the Key Wake Up

1. *Today*, I will plan to use my time wisely with people and causes I deem worthy. I will value the time I have been given and not use any energy toward negativity or areas that *waste my time*. I will begin planning and executing around that plan so I can translate my mission to the daily moments of my life.

2. *Today*, I will accept full responsibility for my life, my thoughts, and my actions. I will think only in terms of how I can improve, how I affect the situations I face, what I feel about others, and how I can contribute to the greater good. I will accept my lot in life and will not project blame on others or my past for where I am today. Today I will choose to become proactive versus reactive to the pressures of life. I will view life as a journey and adventure filled with continuous learning.

3. *Today,* I will no longer run from the facts of my life. I will confront them in all their totality. I will accept the fact that it is what it is and will operate from an environment where the truth is heard. I will listen to my internal voice when seeking guidance, and I will connect to that conscience. I will understand that wherever I am today is not permanent, only temporary, and I will have unwavering faith that I can and will improve and prevail. I will work with a strength from a higher source that teaches us that everything is exactly as it should be.

4. *Today,* I will take a serious inventory of my life in all dimensions: body, mind, heart, and spirit to see where I currently stand. I will ask hard questions such as, "Am I taking care of my body through consistent, repetitive exercise? Am I engaged in continual learning and sharpening of my skills? Do I practice love and work from a passionate perspective in the causes with which I am associated? Am I connected with my source and do I believe in what I'm doing?" Once I take a hard look at my life I will then form action plans to make the necessary changes to get the results I want.

5. *Today,* I will begin the day by getting out of bed when I said I would. I will win the daily private victories by keeping my commitments to myself and others. I will not participate in saying anything negative about another for the entire day. I will set goals and achieve them without wavering because I believe deeply in their contents. I will

educate and obey my conscience by continually seeking
to refine my knowledge, skills, desires, and beliefs.

6. *Today*, I will think deeply about finding and detecting
   my voice. I will ask the questions mentioned in this
   chapter and take a hard look at my present situation. If
   I have not found my voice or if I am in an occupation, I
   will seek to find areas of the job I am passionate about
   or will look at other professions that create a synergy
   between body, mind, heart, and spirit. If I have found
   my voice, I will search for opportunities to give that voice
   away to others and will help and inspire others to find
   their voices. I will value teaching opportunities to impart
   wisdom and knowledge to those I touch and seek to
   transform versus transact with them.

7. *Today*, I will understand that I am the creative force of
   my life. I am the writer of my program and I can live that
   program by design. I will no longer allow others to define
   me and will not worry about social status, the pride of
   being right, or how others portray me. I will work from
   a strong belief in what I'm doing toward a destination I
   deem worthy. I will no longer waste my time or talents in
   causes I do not believe in and will work within my circle
   of influence to do good for the world. I will connect to my
   deepest mission and purpose with a fire that will inspire
   and uplift all my associates. I will become a "creative
   force" that drives good and change in the world.

# Chapter 2 - Dream Up

## Key No. 2 Unlocks the Door to Imagination and Unlimited Possibilities
### *Seven Ways to Dream*

"If one advances confidently in the direction of his dreams and endeavors to live the life he has imagined, he will meet with success unexpected in common hours."

*Henry David Thoreau*

Dreams really do come true. From the time Christine Clifford was a young woman she wanted to be an author. Throughout her youth she cherished writing assignments and looked forward to journalism duties in college. Sidelined by life circumstances she chose to go into the business world and quickly rose to a senior executive vice president of an international marketing company. In 1994 she was diagnosed with breast cancer, a cancer that had spiraled her mother into a deep depression years earlier and caused her father to leave. Christine was determined to use this adversity to accelerate progress versus stagnate movement in her life *(Key No. 5–Pay Up)*. Four weeks following her surgery she awoke in the middle of the night with a vision–cartoons. From there she began intently to read what was available on humor and cancer, and there was very little. She went on to write *Not now, I'm Having a No Hair Day* and *Our Family has Cancer, Too!* Both books became very instrumental in helping to use humor to alleviate the devastation and mental anguish that accompanies cancer. Christine said so eloquently, "Today is a good day to dream." Why should you put off dreaming until tomorrow when you could live out of your imagination today? That imagination will lead you to a better life as long as you break away from the old and into the new.

Paraphrased from *Chicken Soup for the Writer's Soul* (2000)
Jack Canfield, Mark Victor Hansen, Bud Gardner

# 1. Live Out of Your Imagination Instead of Your Memory

Remember this, "A journey requires opening doors that are shut, walking in dark spaces that are frightening, and touching the flame that burns" (Kouzes and Posner, 2002). The question becomes can and will you dream enough to challenge you to go beyond where you currently are? The mind can be transformed. Paulo Coelho wrote, "Each thing has to transform itself into something better and acquire a new destiny." You see, the brain stays elastic throughout life changing itself as we begin to challenge old habits. Studies actually show that the mind has a quarter of a second, called a quarter choice point, in which to catch old, destructive habits before acting on them. We have been granted an unbelievable unique human endowment that animals do not have—imagination. This imagination allows us to create a better world in our minds than what we currently have in virtually every aspect of life. As you begin to live out of your imagination, you begin to see the infinite possibilities of what you could become versus the past conditions of your life or your present reality. For some reason, too many people allow their past actions or circumstances to hold their future success hostage, and I am just not buying it. As I look out over the Pacific Ocean traveling through the outskirts of Canada I see no boundaries, no limitations, and certainly no fear. I only see unlimited opportunity and infinite possibilities. I see miles upon never ending miles of ocean and air. Your life carries the same possibilities—unlimited opportunity. As we become continual learners *(Key No. 3–Clean Up),* we begin to see opportunity everywhere, and we constantly think about ways to improve both our lives and the lives of those around us. We see possibilities, not limitations. Every experience, in every venue, is viewed as a learning experience that gives us more tools, more skills, and more knowledge to build an ever-increasing reservoir of knowledge that can be used at every stop along the journey.

One common denominator that I see among people across the country is that they have created self-imposed prisons and have not grown their imaginations. They are trapped, limiting both their happiness and success. They continually think inside the box, and they have begun to believe that there is nothing bigger for them. This self-imposed prison keeps them exactly where they are and stagnates growth. They have created the very adversity they disdain in their own lives. They want more but have sold their dreams out and simply settled. Well, let me set you straight, our time on earth is much to short to just SETTLE for anything in any compartment of your life. It is time you start thinking big and acting on those thoughts and use the key of imagination to unlock the door to that prison you are in. Go act on those dreams and move in the direction of your imagination and watch what happens. Expect resistance and adversity but if you practice *Key No. 5–Pay Up*, you will just turn that adversity into success.

---

**Imagination Assignment: Take Two Minutes and Think about the Life You Really Want *(Dream Up)***

*"Live out of your imagination instead of your memory"*

---

Sometimes we get so caught up in the activity traps of life just churning out whatever it is we churn out that we seldom take time to really think about our lives. Sure when we see something that moves us or listen to someone who inspires us we do a quick reality check of our situation but then we seldom act on our thoughts. We just think and usually revert back into old patterns of thoughts and actions because it is comfortable. If you were to take just two minutes of totally uninterrupted time right now and think of the three to five things in your life (or many more) that you want to change what would they be? Have you done a life inventory lately just to see if your life is headed anywhere? I believe people are perfectly aligned to get the results they are searching for in their lives. Aim low and you will reach it, aim high and you will reach it as well. My challenge to you today is to live out of your imagination instead of your memory. What you used to be does not matter as the past is finite and the present and future are infinite.

What you can be does matter a great deal. The first step on this journey of self-discovery is figuring out where you are today and understanding this as Einstein said it best, "The significant problems we face today cannot be solved at the same level of thinking we were at when we created them." One definition of insanity would surely be to keep doing what you are doing and expect different results. If you want to change something in your life you must go to a new level of thinking and more importantly, a new level of doing! To go you must first paint a picture in your head of where you want to go and what type of life you aspire to have. You must create a vision of seeing the world through the mind's eye. "Vision is applied imagination" (Covey, 2004). William James said, "Most people live in a very restricted circle of their potential being. We all have reservoirs of energy and genius to draw upon of which we do not dream." I am sure right now you can see yourself lying on a beautiful beach with your significant other (the one you like) and reaping the benefits of all of those great things you have worked so hard to attain in your life. Paint the picture for your life and begin to live from that picture. Without a picture of the person you could be, chances are you will just stay the person you are or what others or society defines you to be. Please remember if you always do what you have always done, then you will always get what you have always gotten. Get the picture? If you do not create a vision, everything will look exactly the same ten years from now with maybe some added pounds.

# 2. Do Not Let Your Past Hold Your Future Hostage

We have all done things in our past of which we are not proud. We all have. "When it's all said and done people will far more regret what they don't do with their lives than what they do with their lives." You may be embarrassed by what you have done. You may not want to replicate it, reproduce it, or relive it, and that's fine. But it was a learning experience and that is all. If you allow something that has happened to you in the past to hinder your thought process, stop you from acting, or keep you from achieving any future success then you have effectively disempowered yourself and allowed the past to hold your future hostage. Folks, the past is finite. It is over. The future is infinite and holds unlimited opportunity. We should be concerned with using our past experiences to build better futures and our wisdom from our failures to help others navigate down life's tough waters, but we should never let it define us. I sincerely believe that we are moving to an age of wisdom. I am currently working on a program titled "The Seven Pillars of Wisdom Leadership." Wisdom helps us navigate down the rocky streams of life because of past experiences. We learn, we grow, and we help others through our own successes and failures.

If people are still judging you based on something that happened in your past, it is their problem, not yours. You don't need those people anyway because they were never really on board with you. People who are mature accept people for who they currently are, not what they used to be. The societal push to judge people based on their past is simply an immature and short-sighted way of thinking. What if all your future accomplishments were put on hold because of things you did in the past? You wouldn't like that would you? I know I wouldn't. Who I am today is not in any way who I used to be, and you are exactly the same way. Every day our knowledge grows and expands, and we should never go back to our past dimensions. It is the beauty of life. It is almost impossible to go backward unless by conscious choice. Make a choice today that you will no longer allow anything you have done in the past define your future potential. Separate where you are today, no matter how low that is, from where you could be. There are countless examples of people that went from nowhere to somewhere because they dreamed and acted. Be one of those people— nothing should be holding back. In the Zen garden of Kyoto you pass through a gate to enter. That gate is referred to as *roji* which symbolizes leaving behind the dust and troubles of the world. When you live out of your imagination you leave behind the past and move into new, unchartered areas of success and significance.

# 3. You Can't Meet New Challenges with Old Ways of Thinking—You Need a New Perspective

I constantly use the saying, "You cannot meet new challenges with old ways of thinking." To go beyond, to reach new arenas of success that you have never experienced before you must simply think and act in new ways that you have never thought before. You must break with the past and use your imagination to create a new and better world for you and those you associate with.

I have been fortunate to coach a women's basketball team that has consistently won twenty plus games a year. That was a good thing but we finally reached a point that did not satisfy anymore. We wanted to grow and expand and do more. I knew what level of work had helped us reach our past successes and the work and thinking it took to get there. To reach a new level of success I knew we would have to act and think in different ways than the past. You can use this mode of thinking to create new results in your own personal and professional life. You know, better than anyone, what has gotten you to where you currently are. You now have a choice to decide if you would like to continue to reach those results or create new results, and this will require new thinking. I constantly challenge all those in our organization to go beyond the past and to develop new actions.

If we have been successful in the past we only figured out what worked up until that day. It does not mean it will be successful today or in the future. It is the past. To move into new arenas of success we have to have fundamental shifts in our thinking by evaluating what we did in the past and changing or upgrading our actions. One definition of insanity that so many people use is "Doing the same things over and over and expecting something different to happen." In *Key No. 1–Wake Up*, I asked you to take a life inventory to see where you currently are. If you were brutally honest about all aspects of your life it would be easy to diagnose why you are where you are. If you don't like where you are or the level of success you have gotten, then you must change the picture by using imagination and creating a new picture and acting from that new picture. You must think in new ways and act on those new thoughts. It is just that simple.

# 4. The Power of Intention— What do you intend today?

The power of intention is strong because from intention flows action. As we begin to understand how to move through *The Belief and Action Model* (Figure 1), we understand the process of believing, seeing, doing, and reflecting. The entire process begins with a basic belief in oneself and from there moves to the arena of creating a vision. From that vision there must be self-discipline to act. This self-discipline is built by winning the private internal battles of your life and garnering the capacity to meet the challenges of the world. This juncture is where most people fail. When your intention is strong enough you will act with unwavering resolve toward your destination, and if you are leading others you will be fanatically driven in the direction of the group's dreams. After completing your objectives it is important to complete the model by reflecting on what you learned and how you can apply the contents to your continuous success. The model is in a circular (continuous) cycle because this process never ends. It is in constant pursuit of reaching and optimizing your potential. If you know anything about potential you know that there is absolutely no way to measure it. Potential is this idea, this concept, of embryonic growth that you will grow and get better everyday from the time you are born until the time you die. The circle of improvement never ends because when it ends, you end. Obviously along the way you can choose not to grow and learn, but that is simply your choice and will result in stagnation and atrophy. The natural consequence of making this choice is that you will become obsolete in the world and will not be rewarded by your actions.

As we match up our internal dialogue with our external actions we begin to create a synergy between our thoughts and our actions resulting in progress, as long as those internal thoughts are positive. We create everything in our life first with our thoughts (intentions) by manifesting those thoughts into actions. When we do not believe in ourselves (doubt) we act from that intention and illuminate insecurity. We attract more into our lives of what we project, therefore attracting minimal amounts of success because of our actions from a paradigm of fear and scarcity. When we have strong internal thoughts of success and significance we then act from those thoughts and attract high energy back into our lives in the form of success and happiness. If you don't believe me, just understand this one concept. Light is positive energy and is much stronger than darkness. If a room is unlit and you turn the lights on, the positive energy overcomes the negative or low energy and lightness overcomes the darkness. Equate this to light being positive and darkness being negative or low energy. What you will find in your life is that when you match positive internal thoughts with external actions you will attract more positive people and things into your life. The light in you will serve to illuminate the good in others and they likewise will reflect that light back to you. This will produce open avenues of communication, respect, and mutual admiration between you and others because you CHOOSE to see the good in them. This will lubricate the process of communication with all you deal with making your life more integrated and complete. Please remember that there are low energy people out there. They are simply acting from their internal thoughts, which are negative. Be a light to those people, not a judge, be a model, not a critic, and your light will overcome their darkness and low energy. You will find that these types of low energy people will simply not want to associate with you and will CHOOSE to find other low energy people in the world and massage each other's hearts why they complain about their lot in life. When you see these people work to illuminate the good in them or choose to disassociate with them, it's your choice. Either way, don't ever forget that you hold the keys to the lock that has either positive or negative energy in it.

# 5. Unleash the Creative Process

Inspiration happens in inspirational places and around inspirational people. As I have stated this throughout the book and if you have read either of my first two books, I mainly write while I vacation in inspirational settings. My first two books were written on the beaches of Florida and much of the content of this book was developed while sailing to Alaska or in cabins in the woods throughout the United States. The entire time, I have been inspired. To revisit, the word inspire means to "breathe life into." There is just something very spiritual that connects to the good and spiritual side of you when you are in nature. Nature flows naturally and with ease. Your life should be the same way, flowing with ease. This doesn't mean there won't be obstacles. By viewing adversity as a means to improve the quality of your life, you change the picture of bad things happening to you to good things happening to you. Many times, we force situations in life when they could just naturally occur if we chose to quit resisting. Deepak Chopra (1994) postulated that everything is exactly the way it should be at this very moment in your life and discussed "The Law of Least Resistance" in his book *Seven Spiritual Laws of Success*. If you accept things as they are and remove judgment, you begin to be fully present in the moment. This in essence will free up energy to enjoy the here and now versus worry about the past or stress over the future. This also refers to unintentional manifestation where things happen in your life because you are simply aligned with your source. You may call this luck but the fact remains that luck favors those who are prepared and who perform consistently. They work from intentional manifestation and because they work from this intention good things happen to them.

To unleash the creativity of your imagination I suggest that you go somewhere that inspires creativity. A park, near water, your back yard, a reading room, the library, around smart people, wherever could inspire YOU to be creative. I regularly meet with creative people to stir ideas and emotions inside me that awaken the creative side I need to be innovative. In everyone's life we become stagnant and need to be awoken and usually this comes by seeing something inspirational or by being around inspired people. Reading is another common avenue to inspiration and opens the imagination to see things multi-dimensionally versus myopically. The important thing is that you regularly include creativity sessions in your life based on your particular lifestyle. This will enrich the process of learning and growing and will make the journey more fun and exciting.

# 6. Expressing Your Voice through Vision and Discipline

Once you have found your voice in life and have some clear direction from Practicing *Key No. 1–Wake Up,* you are on your way to expressing that voice to others in several ways. The first two ways to expression is through the creation of a vision for your life. This vision is seeing the world through the mind's eye and allows you to create a new and exciting path to a better world. Once you have created this vision it places life in the context of a journey, and everyone loves a journey. To reach any destination you must cultivate the discipline to act in the moments of choice to reach that vision. This is the tough part for most people. As suggested earlier, having a life of fulfillment and happiness around passionate execution and significant contribution all flows back to taking full responsibility for your life and your actions, or lack thereof. Between your stimulus and response will be a space and in that space lies your ability to choose. It is from here that self-discipline is built. The word discipline comes from the term "disciple" which means to give yourself to a person or cause. You can effectively become a disciple to yourself winning the private battles necessary to win the public ones. If you do not cultivate this vision or the discipline to act on the vision you will simply remain where you are and time will continue to pass you by.

You cultivate a vision by dreaming, by thinking big, by expanding, and by breaking with old, outdated thought patterns into new ways of living your life. Each year in my organization I create a theme. Last year the theme was "Good to Great" from the popular Jim Collins book. I encouraged my constituents to decide what "Great" looked like. They came up with five things. That was the vision. Everything we did worked backward from that vision. It was a powerful theme because it offered us a mission and a purpose that we could work toward. This year's theme is "The Power of Intention" based on the work of Dr. Wayne Dyer. I will teach from his conclusions and help our people believe that they are worthy of fulfilling their dreams. For me to convince them they are worthy, I must first believe it is a worthy mission and we can fulfill it. From believe stems vision and then you must have the discipline, the execution to complete the vision through repetitive, consistent actions. This will build confidence around the memory of success. Begin today by building a vision of where you are going in your life and start toward that vision by completing and executing the small victories needed to win the ultimate victory. Life is a series of small successes that build up until one day you are a big success. Once you reach a stable level of success (found your voice) you can then begin to search for significance (helping others find their voices).

# 7. Expressing Your Voice through Passion and Conscience

I have not talked much about something I feel adamant about when it comes to living a life of significant contribution, and that is the word passion. Passion is the fuel that drives your car, gets you excited, rows your boat, and helps you to dig down deep to find meaning among chaos in your life. Passion defined is an irresistible belief for motive or action. Without passion, life is dull and mundane. With it life is exciting and adventurous. As I travel the country I have discovered that lots of people are lacking passion. Because of this lack of love from the heart (passion), people plod through jobs, relationships, friendships, and any other endeavor they decide to undertake. To be great at anything I firmly believe you have got to have passion for it. I started writing books and speaking because I had a deep desire to help others fulfill their potential in life by encouraging them to act. This passion started in coaching but then manifested into speaking, consulting, and writing. As I traveled the world I begin to see what I said lit the inner fire among individuals everywhere and I could see their eyes shine. This affirmation only fueled my passion for exploring the field of personal growth and organizational effectiveness because I knew that the only way to grow an organization was to grow the people. In the process I understood that you simply could not have one without the other. I also knew the tremendous amount of personal growth that I had experienced through educating my mind and heart and the benefits my organization had garnered because of it. From that I knew I HAD to share my gift with others. I hope my passion for continual growth is contagious and has rubbed off on you. If you want those you associate with to be passionate about anything, you must first model the behavior you want from them. Remember, be a light of passionate behavior, not a critic, be a model, not a judge. Illuminate the light on others and maybe in the process they will begin to feel the spirit move within them. The word inspiration comes from "spirit within" and the word enthusiasm derives from "god within." Help others feel the spirit and god within them. When thinking about what you specifically need to do with your life (find your voice) ask this question, "What is it that I cannot not do?" Replace the question with, "What do I need to do with the previous question and you will get closer to finding your voice.

Conscience is that internal voice that longs to connect to something larger and the need to leave a legacy and live a life of deep meaning and significant contribution. In order to do this you must begin the exploration process of finding your voice so you can inspire others to find theirs. Once we find our voices in our vocations and understand that most of the good that is done in the world is in and through organizations, we begin to place our time, talents, and energy in organizations that we believe in and for causes we deem worthy. One person, however, can make a significant difference in the world by continually growing his or her influence and deeply impacting others. Through emotional identification what we have to say can strongly resonate with others in such a way that truly transforms lives. Many of you have been transformed by something you read or saw on TV. This emotional identification is so strong it actually feels like you know the people who are influencing you. It is important that we continually expand and educate our conscience and develop the capacity to listen to it in tough moments of choice. This will be our guide to wisdom and clarity and help us stay out of personal and professional tough spots. Try for just one day to listen to your conscience and connect the dots of what it is trying to urge you to do. Develop the internal discipline to act on that conscience and see how much better you feel about the results.

# Chapter 2 Summary— Seven Action Items to Manifest the Key Dream Up

1. *Today,* I will live out of my imagination instead of my memory. I will consciously spend thirty minutes reflecting on my life in four areas: body, mind, heart, and spirit and will focus on improving my skills, knowledge, desire, and beliefs. Today I will plan a trip to a place that resonates with me so my mind and heart are awakened to the beauty

of life. Today, I will spend time reflecting and focusing on my dreams.

2. *Today*, I will forgive myself for my past transgressions. I will realize that all people have made poor decisions in the past and I will allow those past decisions to serve as a light of positive energy to my future. I will forgive those who have transgressed against me and hurt me and lose the burden of revenge in my heart. I will not be ashamed of my past decisions or wallow in regret as I fully understand that only when I use those decisions for future improvement are they beneficial to me and others. I will start today off with a fresh slate and allow others the opportunity to start fresh with me. I will understand that life is much too short to allow my past (in any area of my life) to hold my future hostage.

3. *Today*, I will fully understand that I cannot meet new challenges or reach new successes with old, outdated ways of thinking. I will think and act in new ways and empower myself to think big and act on those thoughts. Through an active inventory of my life I will investigate what rendered past results and work to create new results based on new knowledge and new concepts. Today, I will spend time sharing and garnering new knowledge that will make me a commodity in the workplace. I will focus on solutions versus problems. Today, I will think in ways I've never thought before and see life in ways I've never seen

it before. I will become the light to others that illuminates and radiates constant and continual growth.

4. *Today,* I will understand that actions come from intentions. I will examine my thoughts and my internal dialogue to match positive thoughts with positive actions and will work diligently to create congruence with my mission and my moments of life. I will work from an intention to manifest positive thoughts while all the time knowing that good things will happen to me if I move confidently in the direction of my dreams. Today, I will intend to make a difference in the lives of others and will fully understand my role as an important part of the whole.

5. *Today,* I will unleash the creative process by spending time reflecting. I will go to a place where I can stop and think and connect to my source of inspiration. I will understand that inspiration happens in inspirational settings and around inspirational people. I will model inspiration around those I associate with fully understanding that I have a choice between stimulus and response and choose how I respond to the many stimuli I face on a daily basis. Today, I will visit with others who inspire and uplift me and choose to disassociate with those who project negative draining energy.

6. *Today*, I will express my voice through vision and discipline. I will consciously examine where I am going with my life and will see the world through the mind's eye. I will "walk my talk" and will begin to build the self-discipline and capacity to act in the daily moments of life. I will fully realize that to reach a destination, it must first be designed, and I will align both my thoughts and actions so I can reach that destination. Today I will move with purpose and intention toward my dreams and will act on three high-value (action items that yield optimum results) activities toward that destination.

7. *Today*, I will act with passion and conscience to express my voice. Today, I will move with fire and intent and will live "inspired." Today, I will work with a fervor and drive uncommon to ordinary people and will be driven by my conscience, my sense of meaning and purpose in life. Today, I will reflect on my vocation and truly see if it intersects with my passion and conscience. Today, I will practice compassion for others and will fully understand that I have the power to be a tremendous creative force in the world. Today, I will live life to the fullest without negativity, jealously, scarcity, or anger.

# Chapter 3 - Clean Up

## Unlocks the Door to Inner Peace and Successful Projection

*Seven Areas to Refine in your Life*

As I begin this chapter I want to share a story from my life to illustrate the concept of cleaning up. Recently I made a conscious decision to rid myself of the worry of what others think about me. Stop and reflect for a moment on your own life and how you have allowed others to define you and criticize you in ways that have shaped your decisions and defined your own self-worth. Unfortunately we live in a society that promotes pushing others down to get where we're going. Deep within each of us is a need to be loved and accepted but we must first love and accept ourselves internally before we can return that love back to others, even to those who transgress against us.

Have you ever been in a room or with others who claim to be your friends only to feel the judging, the comparing, the jealously, or the contentious spirit they bring to the conversation. Just yesterday I was with a group of people where this spirit of downgrading, demeaning, and competition dominated the air. I discussed this concept with another person and he said to me that there were basically two groups of people; acquaintances and friends and he could count on one hand his true friends. I refuted that concept and shared with him that I thought there were three levels of interaction with others: acquaintances, friends, and advocates. Acquaintances are people you speak to, know little about, but could become friends. Friends are people who you have shared experiences with—either positive or negative—and could be called upon to help in a situation if it was possible for them. But advocates are people with whom you have shared a lot with and would never judge you or criticize you for your actions. Advocates will always support you especially in times of your absence. Stephen Covey said so eloquently, "If you want to retain those who are present, be loyal to those who are absent." We simply lose trust and credibility with everyone when we judge and criticize.

That experience awakened something inside me and helped me to see that we should never allow others to define us, because they will in non-threatening ways to them, and more importantly we should rid ourselves of the worry associated with just friends. More important than that concept is that we never become those people that judge, criticize, ridicule, compare, compete, contend, or seek to belittle. We have got two choices in life—one is to take the road to mediocrity which is the road most traveled, the other is to take the road to greatness and meaning. The beauty of life is that you get to choose which road you take. Just make sure you choose wisely. Decide today to cleanse your life of the toxins that will never help you get where you truly deserve to go and be more concerned with building stark raving crazy advocates than just friends.

# 1. Understand and Value Your Self-Worth

You are here for a specific reason on this earth. You are valuable and have the same needs everyone else has to

Live - The body's need
Love - The heart's need
Learn - The mind's need
Leave a Legacy- The spirit's need

As you begin to tap into your birth gifts you realize that you gain in internal value when you live your life in service to others. So many people I come in contact with have de-valued themselves because of what others have said to them (environment), what has happened to them (psychological), or they have experienced some sort of failure and allowed the past to hold their future hostage, as mentioned before. You should never, ever treat yourself second class because the moment you do, you encourage others to do the exact same thing. Many times, only confidence, is the deciding factor that separates one success story from a failure. Confidence can be defined as the memory of success and you garner success through belief, vision, action, and reflection (The Manifestation Model).

I fully realize that many of us live from the social mirror (allowing others opinions of us to dictate how we feel about ourselves) but confidence can be entirely internal and flows from the memory of success. We garner success through consistent and repetitive repetition. When we allow others to define us based on their opinions of us or their actions toward us, we effectively disempower ourselves and empower their weakness to control us. When we live our life around values and self-evident principles, they can become our lighthouses and can offer our internal spring of confidence to work toward our dreams. To truly reach an inner peace, you must clearly define the values in which you want to live by, work in the directions of your dreams with a passion, and don't ever de-value what you are doing. All those people who may laugh at you on the front end will be converted to believers on the back end. Remember, talk is cheap, but action will make believers out of disbelievers.

# 2. Change Your Internal Dialogue

What are you telling yourself right now? I'm not good enough, I'm not smart enough, I'm not good looking enough,

I'm not thin enough? These are all reactive responses to the social mirror of society. For us to change what we feel on the outside we have to train ourselves to clean up our internal language so that it accurately reflects a confidence in ourselves that can drive our actions. Low self-esteem stems from a lack of belief in oneself which flows from our internal dialogue. When we change the internal picture we know that we do have something unique to offer, can constantly grow in areas of deficiency, and can build confidence through repetition. This internal emotional strength is similar to building physical strength. How do you build physical strength? You lift weights consistently, you run consistently, you exercise consistently. You build emotional strength exactly the same way, through consistent deposits into your own emotional bank account. You win the private battles of your soul by making and keeping commitments to yourself and to others. You hold yourself accountable, you build integrity, and you translate your mission daily in the tough moments of choice. You educate and obey your conscience by living a principle-centered life. One of the strongest ways to find yourself and build your internal dialogue is to immerse yourself in service to others. As you illuminate the good in others you will light your own fire, recognize the value you have to offer, and reaffirm the worth and potential in yourself. Remember, one definition of leadership is communicating and validating the worth and potential in others in so clearly a way that they begin to see it in themselves. My first piece of advice is to start with yourself.

# 3. Begin Everything with a Belief in Self and in the Cause

Everything begins with belief. Even before you can see anything in your life you must first believe that a better world can exist. Vision tied to discipline to act followed by reflection follows (refer to The Belief Model 1). Notice that I said that belief must be in self first and in the cause second. Every humanistic organizational problem begins at the personal level and stems from dysfunctionality with self. If you do not believe in yourself and have not developed your "voice" it will be very difficult to lend that voice to a cause you deem worthy. If you have found your voice and have found a cause you believe in then you are well on your way to contributing your unique voice to a cause you deem worthy. At the intersection of talent, passion, needs of the world, and conscience lies most likely your vocation in life. When we go to work in jobs and do not believe in ourselves we neglect the mind, heart, and spirit of ourselves and treat ourselves second class. This usually results in giving others permission to treat us second class. They can see that we have not paid the emotional price to security and confidence and that we do not value ourselves. This red light will get you passed over every time as you try to move up the food chain and will lead to discontent in both yourself and in your job.

The second part of this equation is belief or lack thereof in the causes you choose to spend your time in. Much of the legacy you will leave in your life will be in and through the organizations in which you choose to participate. If you do believe fully in the cause and the vision of the cause then you will most likely engage all dimensions (body, mind, heart, and spirit) to that cause. You will give of your whole self. This is really what we are trying so desperately to do in the knowledge worker era. Our goal is to unleash the latent and undeveloped potential in all our people. In essence, help them find their voices in life. When you do not believe in the cause you work for both your heart and your spirit will be neglected because the principles go against your conscience. This lack of congruence will produce feelings of discontent and you will be unhappy and unfulfilled with the cause. If you have ever heard anyone refer to having a "broken spirit" or "lost passion" in their job, it's a manifestation of neglecting the heart and the spirit. Similar feelings persist in your personal life if you associate with people that live from different principles than you. You can either change what you value (reactive) or have the emotional strength to stand up for what you believe in (proactive). You must do this with balance of both courage and consideration for the other person and this normally defines your personal maturity level. In my second book *The Inspirational Leader*, I noted that people want to wake up in the morning and go to a job they love, for a cause they deem worthy, and for a leader in whom they can believe. When you find that synergistic mix you will be in an environment that optimizes and unleashes the human potential inside you. If you are not currently in that position, you probably stay in a funk, do not believe in the mission or leader of the organization, and get all of your satisfaction off the job. The challenge with this way of thinking is that the largest percentage of your life will be spent working. Remember the needs of people based on a holistic approach to living (body to live, mind - to learn, heart - to love, spirit - to leave a legacy). Finding your voice in life and in your vocation will lead to significant contribution and passionate execution around what matters most to you.

# 4. Get Rid of the Toxins in Your Life

I do not know any other way to say this, "Lose the negativity in your life." That means the negative internal thoughts, the negative people around you, the negative things you tolerate, the reactiveness from both you and the people around you, all of it. To live a life of happiness you must build the emotional strength to take full responsibility for your life and decide what you will tolerate and what you will not. As you build that emotional strength you will build an immune system to negative people and circumstances. In fact we attract back into our life what we put out, so if you are positive and proactive you will most likely attract positive and proactive people back into your life. Negative people will see your positive behavior as kryptonite and run in the other direction. Your stimulus will create the very response you are looking for. Have you ever tried to be mad at someone who will not be mad back? Have you ever tried to stay upset with someone who just moves on? Have you ever tried to argue with someone who will not argue back? Frustrating huh? You be the light that illuminates the good in others. The hardest thing you will ever have to do is see the good in people and radiate and affirm that good. The easy thing to do is to compare, criticize, complain, contend, and compete for self-worth and potential through bad-mouthing, undermining, trash talking, or a continual demeaning of another's spirit. Listen and feel to the heart and soul of others as they communicate to you. This psychological air and space you give them will affirm and validate the worth and potential in them in clear ways that will illuminate the positive and hide the negative.

For some reason many of us allow negative people to drain the very positive energy we have. This is a reactive response to the world and disempowers us and gives our power to their weaknesses. There is certainly enough negativity in the world, and you can be drawn into it if you CHOOSE to, but successful people are not negative people. The best people understand that when they use their position of power in negative ways to get things done that they are borrowing strength from a formal position. This is based on a paradigm of fear and insecurity. This will build weakness in the relationship in two ways: in self (because you used your formal power to coerce someone into acting) and in others (because you bullied them into acting). Moral authority, where people openly choose to follow you, is a much better avenue from which to act. This area to refine is simple. Decide today that you will not allow the moods or feelings of others to steal away your internal strength and confidence. Practice being a light, not a judge, a model, not a critic.

# 5. Become a Continual Learner and Constantly Educate Yourself

The key to unlimited opportunity is through education. Knowledge, if used properly, can truly become influence. When I refer to educating yourself in both my lectures and in my books I don't necessarily mean going back to college. That option simply is not for everyone, but young people who have the opportunity should strongly look at these figures:

> *The average college graduate will make over $600,000 in his or lifetime over a person who does not attend college.*

If college or continuing a formal education is not an option for you, then the key is to constantly want to grow in your particular field and to grow your knowledge base. This adds tremendous value to your life and the organization's life and makes you a hot commodity. As you constantly learn new trends in your field your mind will be challenged, you will be inspired, and you will begin to share your knowledge with others. This also helps in your pursuit of being the best at what you do. Remember, the mind's need is to constantly learn and grow and this can only be completed by challenging its current boundaries. My own learning did not accelerate until I was 25 years old and from that point forward I wanted to read everything I could get my hands on. I became a sponge for learning and growth. My friends and family could not understand why I constantly wanted to learn. I simply told them I was deeply passionate about personal growth, being the best in my fields, and sharing my new found knowledge with others. The best investment I ever made was pursuing both my master's and doctorate degrees. Both of those experiences were transformational and lit my fire of learning and growing. There are many ways to learn in this information era such as online education, seminars, the exchange of knowledge and ideas with your cohorts, the Internet, mentoring, educational TV, and reading. Just by picking up this book and reading this far, you have made an internal choice to improve yourself.

I shared earlier with you that the mind is elastic and grows when it is challenged. You must begin the process of challenging that mind. How can you do this? It is simple. You can read, listen to educational CDs, attend seminars, speak to the best in your field, share knowledge with others, or do anything that challenges you to think. If you are truly in your passion area for your vocation, you will not have to be pushed to want to learn. Thomas Friedman (2006) in *The World is Flat* said," Nobody works harder at learning than a curious kid." If you want to continue learning you have to become curious about something. I hope it is your field or vocational area. Friedman also has a formula for success—CQ + PQ > IQ. CQ stands for Curious Quotient, PQ for Passion Quotient, and IQ for Intellect Quotient. He simply believes that a passionate person who is curious is a much better hire any day than a purely intellectual person. I tend to agree. I would take a person who is curious and has built high levels of emotional intelligence and who has passion any day in the workplace.

Not seeking to learn will breed complacency, and complacency will never place you among the elite in your category. You must intend to be the best and work backward from that intention. To do that becoming a continual learner is simply part of the process. Also, as you learn more you will begin to transcend one market and your skills will make you accessible for more jobs and will open you up to a better financial life. When you do not learn, you choose to pigeon hole yourself into one profession and lock the door on what could be a self-imposed prison for many years. Remember, the average person will spend 45 percent of his/her life working. That is a long time to get up and go to a job you do not love and your heart is not into. When you don't educate yourself, you could be locking yourself into that job for a long time. The new era is built around "knowledge workers" who constantly grow and learn.

# 6. Change the Picture about What You Do for a Career (Job, Career, Vocation)

If I were to ask you what you do for a profession today, what would you tell me? Many times when I speak I ask that question and I almost always get the same responses: I'm a nurse, a supervisor, a manager, a crew leader, a factory worker, etc. Then I ask them what they really do for a living? They become frustrated when I continue to probe them for an answer. When I ask that question of a nurse at one of my lectures she finally said, "Look, I help people when they are sick, okay?" I said, "Do you save people's lives?" She said, "Yes." I said, "Do you help people at their most uncomfortable times in life?" She said, "Yes." Well then, I said, "You have got a whole lot bigger reason for waking up in the morning than to just be nurse or to pick up a paycheck." What is it that you really do for a living? I could give you the standard answer that I'm a coach, a speaker, an author, an athletic director, and a consultant. And that would be very generic. But what I really wake up in the morning to do is to spotlight the potential in others, speak to people to create enthusiasm and action toward significance, write books to inspire others to become their best, lead people toward a vision in an athletic department, and enable greatness in organizations across the country. Those are bigger reasons to get up and go to work in the morning and are integrated into my whole life. They permeate my existence and give me meaning and purpose. This lifestyle is not compartmentalized but rather integrated around what I love doing.

My challenge to you today is to change the picture of what you do for a living and to see that profession as not only a means to a financial end, but also a journey of self-discovery and service to others. If you do not believe in the cause you go to work for everyday or the people you do it with then find another cause. Remember *Key No. 1–Wake Up* unlocks the door to taking responsibility for your life and that includes the vocation you choose to participate in. Many of you most likely got into your profession because you loved a certain aspect of it in the beginning. You had passion and enthusiasm. You must always reconnect to that passion, especially if you have lost it. Find a big reason to wake up and go to it every morning, and you'll begin to see your life as being integrated around what you love. This will add more fulfillment to your life and add a much needed meaning and purpose. The key is to search and work to make the transition from effectiveness to greatness daily.

# 7. Project Success on Your Movie Screen

Ninety-three percent of all communication is non-verbal. Every time we walk in a room, sit in a chair, sit in a meeting, look at another, or just be we are communicating with others. Can you tell what others have on their minds when they are around, and they do not even have to say a word? Can you tell when there are ulterior motives and hidden agendas based on the actions of others? If you want to live a life of deep meaning and significant contribution you have to learn to project success on your own personal movie screen. Some of you could be wondering why what you project to others has to do with your own professional success. As we move up the continuum and begin to practice *Key No. 6—Build Up*, we see that the only way to significance is through others. To do this we have to project positive vibes. Those vibes will always come back to us through the aforementioned power of intention. As I travel the country speaking to all types of people there are certain universal principles that always apply. Smiling will almost always result in a smile back. Please and thank you will always make the person who offered the service feel better, and a healthy positive attitude will always go further than a negative one.

In the workplace movers and shakers rarely have time for negative attitudes or projections of people who are not on board. Leaders are looking for individuals who realize that life is not always easy and the best way to predict the future is to create it. Once you have climbed the ladder of success, as many of you will, don't ever forget that now you have more influence and can do more good than you previously could. Never underestimate the power of positive projections. There's nothing that can turn someone who's a big fan off quicker than a negative attitude. Start today by becoming aware of what you're projecting on your movie screen and change the picture if it's negative. I know many people who have developed a functional blindness to their own defect of projecting negativity. When others let you in on the secret that you have a bad attitude, take heed to the advice .

# Chapter 3 Summary— Seven Action Items to Manifest the Key Clean Up

1. *Today*, I will value my self-worth. I will not allow anyone's judgments, criticism, or negative thinking to limit my future potential. Today, I will accept the fact that I have made mistakes and transgressed against others. I will live today with happiness in my heart and will accept myself and others as they are. I will treat myself first class in all things I do and will begin every endeavor with a belief in self and in cause.

2. *Today*, I will change my internal dialogue to one that values and appreciates my uniqueness. I will understand that I am special, have many talents to offer, and will constantly affirm my own worth and potential. I will pay the price to build emotional security so I can decide what my own worth is, not how others define me.

3. *Today*, I will begin everything I do with a belief in self and cause. I will have this belief because I fully know that I have built emotional strength through consistent repetition and practice. Today, I will only choose to participate in things that I believe in and will choose to disassociate with the causes that are not in alignment with my heart and spirit and in areas from which I am not passionate. I will seek to create a synergy between my talents, passions, needs of the world, and my conscience that will manifest meaning and contribution. Today, I will believe and dream again if I have lost my voice.

4. *Today*, I will complete a personal inventory and cleanse my life of the toxins present. This may be with a job, a friendship, a relationship, or a cause. No longer will I allow others to define me. Today, I will experience an awakening of life and energy and will work with purpose, passion, presence, and perseverance toward my dreams. Today, I will take out the trash and not look back. I will work to make positive deposits into the emotional bank

accounts of others through service and contribution. Today, I will become less interested in making friends and more interested in building stark-raving crazy advocates.

5. *Today*, I will make a choice to fight the emotional cancer of complacency. Today, I will not allow myself to stagnate or fall victim to atrophy. Today, I will make the most important investment I can and that is an investment in self. Today, I will make a conscious choice to become a constant, continual learner. Today, I will seek opportunities to grow and expand through the sharing of knowledge, meaningful conversations, and reading. Today, I will search for opportunities to attend seminars or learn from the best in the world. Today, I will grow and never return to my previous dimensions.

6. *Today*, I will change the picture about what I do for a living. I will no longer see my job as a means to a financial end. Today, I will seek to serve, contribute, execute, and believe in the mission of the organization. Today, I will awake up with a purpose, a vision, a passion, and an intention to improve the greater good through my talents. Today, I will make a difference in the world and in the lives of those I interact with. Today, I will find my voice in my current job and move toward significance. Today, I will work with a fervor that will radiate purpose in the workplace.

7. *Today*, I will grow my self-awareness to fully realize
   what I project on my movie screen. Today, I will radiate
   positive energy, I will illuminate the positive in others,
   and I will allow negative energy to bounce off of me.
   Today, I will fully understand how important attitude
   is to success and I will seek to reward positive attitudes
   from those around me. Today, I will fully understand
   that leadership is a choice, just as a positive disposition
   is, and I will seek to communicate and validate the
   potential in others in so clearly a way that they begin to
   see it in themselves. Today, I will be light that overtakes
   the darkness of cynicism and negativity. Today, I will
   model the behavior I want from others.

# Chapter 4 - Listen Up

## Key No. 4 Unlocks the Door to Wisdom and Living a Conscience-Driven Life
### Seven Concepts to Hear

Just this past year I began to use the terminology of *becoming humble and teachable* as a way to show how learning begins. This saying originated one day at my office while I was discussing the six emotional cancers with my players. I was outlining which emotional cancer was the most prevalent in each player's grade level. I happened to have a senior in my office, and I said, "This is simple. You have the knowledge, the skills, and the belief in yourself and the cause. The biggest battle you will fight daily is maintaining a burning desire to compete at the highest levels. The emotional cancer you will face will simply be complacency." Many of you that are reading this book have been in jobs for long periods of time and have allowed yourself to stagnate and become a victim of atrophy. You, too, are facing the emotional cancer of complacency.

As I shared that statement, the next statement came out of my mouth, "You must remain humble and teachable and fully understand that the more knowledge we garner the more we grow our circle of ignorance. We do this because we come to the realization that there are so many things that we still have to learn." From that day forward I have used that in both my life and the life of my organization. When you stop learning, you stop growing and if you ever reach a point of arrogance to really believe that you know everything there is to know you effectively make yourself obsolete in the market.

In this chapter I will discuss the key of listening to the voices all around you. I will encourage you first to listen to your conscience, that small, still voice inside you that, if educated properly, will steer you toward congruence and alignment with your spirit and source. I will also encourage you to form your own board of directors, a group of people who can offer wisdom at the crossroads of your life. I'm convinced that we are moving to an age of wisdom. As Peter Senge (2004) wrote in *Presence*, "As complexity increases, the need for wisdom grows, even as our wisdom atrophies." Don't fall victim to complacency. Seek and listen to those wise voices around you and make every week an upward spiral of effective living and learning.

# 1. Be Quiet and Listen to Your Conscience

The next time you are making a big decision between your stimulus and response simply be quiet and listen. Listen to what you ask? Your conscience. Your conscience is your internal voice that steers you toward good decisions in your life and away from bad ones. There is a mass of evidence that suggests that conscience, a moral sense, is a universal phenomenon and transcends all religions and boundaries. Immanual Kant once said, "I am constantly amazed by two things; the starry heavens above and the moral law within." Conscience, if educated properly, can become that moral law within. Some people believe, as author Stephen Covey does, that it is the voice of God to his children. When you listen to your conscience it drives your actions and reflects both the good in you and the good in others. It illuminates principles of honesty, fairness, integrity, love, kindness, and positive thoughts.

Conscience is a small, still voice within you, and it is associated with positive things. Ego, on the other hand, is social mirror driven, large, and dictatorial. It focuses on the needs of self first and is not concerned with the well-being of others. It drives one to search to meet ends in any possible way even if that way is underhanded, dirty, or duplicitous with one's moral behavior. Ego straightjackets potential and seeks to disempower others and is threatened by any negative feedback. It even punishes those who offer advice and feedback.

Conscience is the opposite, it values feedback as feed forward, and seeks to empower and unleash the creativeness and innovating side in others.

This is a simple one. Listen to your conscience. Avoid your ego at all cost. Ego will cost you friends and loved ones. Begin today to live in congruence with your conscience. As your heart and mind steer you toward something, listen and act. This synergy between what is deeply important to you (conscience) and your actions will create alignment and congruence with your deepest source.

# 2. Form Your Own Board of Directors

Your life is sacred and important. Wise counsel can help you avoid a life of heartache and pitfalls. To help with major life planning as it relates to your personal life, professional life, financial matters, and direction you should form your own board of directors (BOD). This body should consist of people who are your advocates. The difference between an advocate and a friend is essential. An advocate has your back in all situations and would never do anything to devalue your relationship. An advocate would stand up for you when you are absent if others were negative about you and would be the first to tell you if you were involved with things or people that could potentially harm your well-being. Much of friendships and relationships today are built around convenience. Friends may only be there for you when it's a good time for them, may allow others to talk about you behind your back, and may secretly wish for you to fail, but never an advocate. Now that we've discussed the important differences between advocates and friends let's look at your board.

Your board should be between three and five people. These people should have many life experiences in both failure and defeat and should have both the character and competence you need to trust them at deep levels. They should have reached some level of success in their own lives and are consistent with backing up what they say. Once they have built this integrity, you will trust their judgment. You will meet with these people as many times as once a quarter, possibly over dinner, or a minimum of two times per year. Here are some areas you should discuss and seek guidance:

1. Career goals, redefining of those goals, and reasonable benchmarks
2. Relationships
3. Spirituality
4. Support for new challenges in your life
5. Grief periods after loss in your life
6. Motivation before embarking on new journeys
7. Financial matters
8. The open exchange of knowledge and wisdom

These are only eight, but I think a critical eight. Obviously you could call emergency meetings (just like a real board) as needed but this is a time to "Listen Up" and take good notes. Many of the true advocates we have in our life truly want us to be successful and will help navigate us down uncertain waters in life. They care and want the best for us. Many times you will not want to hear what they have to say but it is vitally important to create an environment where the truth is heard and they simply don't just tell you what you want to hear. These sessions should last anywhere from two to six hours and should be planned. Start today by identifying your own board of directors and shave off years of learning by avoiding the "school of hard knocks."

# 3. Redefine Feedback to Feed Forward and Realize It Is a Gift

Part of listening up is to redefine what feedback is. Unfortunately, in our scarcity minded society where we believe in win-lose thinking, much of the feedback that is given from one group to another is negative and construed that way. Because of that we tend to tune it out as a personal attack on our character. If we could redefine the word feedback to feed forward and search for the grains of truth in every comment we get from another we become proactive to the words and not reactive. Sure, there is some feedback that is malicious and has a negative connotation but as we continue to educate ourselves we see that everyone is approaching every situation from their unique perspective. Many times the gaps in paradigms between two people allow for the biggest opportunities for disagreement. If we viewed those gaps as opportunities for synergy and creativity versus gaps of disagreement, we would be a whole lot better off.

Change the picture of what feedback is to that of a gift. That gift if viewed properly could be the best gift you ever received. I will address this concept later when I discuss using adversity to accelerate progress *(Key No. 5–Pay Up)* but just for a moment think about all the things said to you in your life that you found hurtful and resentful. I bet your heart was involved in those things. This could have come in the form of a significant other breaking up with you or a co-worker that you thought you had a great relationship with slamming you. Either way, it may have hurt. At the seed or root of those comments could have been some truth that you did not recognize and it only illuminated the truth to you about the other person. You don't deserve to be in a relationship where the other person doesn't love you and you do not want to have to count on someone who is not reliable because they do not believe in you. A dear friend of mine and very wise woman named Kelly Lavender always says to me, "When people try and show you who they are, you should always believe them." I say sometimes, "What you are shouts so loudly, I cannot hear what you have to say." Either way, people are constantly showing us who they are and if we can trust them. Learn to change the picture about what feedback is and see it as a very valuable gift you need to know to move in the next direction. Make a decision to associate and spend your time only with people who have your best interest at heart. Then, you know the feed back is for your best interest and not theirs.

# 4. Find and Listen to as Many Smart People as You Can

How do you grow beyond your past limitations into new arenas of success? You have to expand, challenge your current way of thinking, and be willing to get out of the boat. One sure way to grow in any area of your life is by finding and listening to as many smart people as you can. Set up monthly meetings with people where you can share knowledge and be inspired. Remember, that word inspire means to breathe into. There are certain people in my life that I meet with regularly in each arena where we share knowledge and ideas about current trends, what works and what doesn't, and new techniques, principles, or strategies of success. In the coaching business I keep a network of the best that I can call to "pick their brains." I have the same in the speaking and consulting business. These conversations illuminate and validate the belief and potential in what I'm doing and usually stir something in me that awaken my inner fire. Just as a board of directors helps you both personally and professionally in certain general areas, these people are experts in their field and help grow your competence.

This is one important habit to cultivate. Stephen Covey (1989) calls it the habit of renewal named "Sharpen the Saw." We must all learn to sharpen our saw in all dimensions including:

1. Body
2. Mind
3. Heart
4. Spirit

By listening and drinking deeply from the knowledge of others we hone our own skills in all four dimensions. The next step is to take the newfound knowledge, act on it, and then share it with as many people as you can. Only scarcity minded people hoard information and don't share with others. Individuals who believe in abundance share with others everything they know. Start today by finding those smart people and listen up!

# 5. Become Humble and Teachable

This is a very critical point to learning. To learn anything you must first become both humble and teachable. As a basketball coach, I constantly use the saying, "The teacher cannot teach until the pupil is ready." This simply means that until a player is ready to be taught no learning will occur. Many times in life we create the very adversity we are facing by becoming filled with venom and pride. Remember, "pride goeth before a fall." Pride stems from ego and is in direct contrast with conscience. When we believe that we know everything there is to know, that very thought limits our growth. Intelligent people understand that as our circle of knowledge grows so does our circle of ignorance. You see, the more we know the more we realize we don't know. If you remember this concept you will be in a perpetual state of learning and growing, wanting to retain and act on as much information as possible.

The very second you think you know everything or that you can't learn anything from another, you have created a roadblock to your learning. If you are in an organization and you are a leader in that organization most likely you will want all of your people to learn and grow. The best example you can give to those people is to model the way. If you want them to learn, let them see you learn and grow. If you want them to become humble and teachable, let them see you become humble and teachable. Seek first the benefit of others versus your own benefit and watch your relationships grow and expand.

# 6. The Answers Are All Around You

They always tell us that when there is a fire we should look, listen, and roll. Well, in this setting of listening and learning you should also look, listen, and roll. Look at the example of others around you. Constantly study people and what makes them successful or unsuccessful. Read, listen, go to lectures, talk with others, watch body language, watch educational TV, and constantly evaluate others. Look to see what makes things work or not. Many times the answers come to us by watching others fail. Listen to those around you. Listen to wise counsel. Listen to your board of directors. Listen to your advocates. Listen to your inner voice. Just be quiet and listen. And finally, roll. Roll with the punches. Roll with adversity. Roll with setback. Roll with heartache. Roll with negativity. Just roll with it!

The point here is simple. We live in an information overloaded society. If you really want to grow and expand the answers are simply ALL around you. All you have to do is listen and learn to grow and expand. Start today by listening and observing twice as much as you speak. We have two eyes and two ears and only one mouth for a reason. I think the good Lord was trying to tell us something with that.

# 7. Listen to Your Internal Compass as It Relates to Your Vocation

I come across so many people who have so many wonderful ideas about their lives. Between them thinking and them doing many times is a space and in that space lies their ability to choose their response to virtually any situation they have. (I will revisit turning thought into action with *Key No. 7—Act Up,* but for now just think.) When I ask people to talk about their passion, they immediately speak from their hearts because they are listening to their conscience. Just this moment as I overlook the beautiful water outside Ketchikan, Alaska, on the way to Victoria, Canada, I am overwhelmed with passion. As I write, the words seem to just flow naturally because I know that upon completion of this book the contents will help people from all walks of life to act on their hopes and dreams and prevent them from living lives of quiet desperation. I know when I am speaking and coaching and consulting that I am right where I need to be at that moment. The joy and pleasure that I get from acting on my inner hopes brings both happiness and fulfillment to my life. It helps me to fully understand that *this ain't no practice life* and that we should all be able to experience fully passionate execution and significant contribution. We should all be able to wake up in the morning and go to a job we love, for a cause we deem worthy, and for a leader in whom we can believe.

As we listen to our inner hearts and act from those intentions we begin to create a synergy between our heart and our mind and create an inner peace that both calms and excites at the same time. It is the ultimate synergistic process and what Covey calls "the sweet spot." Many of you have experienced this "sweet spot" in your vocations and can relate to what I am saying, but far too many have not found this "sweet spot" and long for it. By following the seven keys in this book, you are well on your way to living a life that matters because your life will be integrated around what you love. Now that we have you where you need to be, we have to teach you how to reach your dreams. Listen up!

# Chapter 4 Summary— Seven Action Items to Manifest the Key Listen Up

1. *Today*, I will stop, be completely quiet, and listen to my conscience. I will follow the inner wisdom of my conscience. Today, I will be fully aware of how I treat others and notice if that treatment is in congruence with my inner spirit. I will seek to build others up versus tear others down. I will seek to illuminate the potential in myself and in others. Today, I will reflect on life by

asking what my conscience would do in all situations. I will then act from that still, small voice that points me toward right and wrong.

2. *Today*, I will begin thinking who I would like to join my board of directors. I will search for people who care deeply about me, illuminate the potential in me, and build me up. Today, I will seek to find and listen to these individuals who offer hope, faith, and wisdom and care deeply that I make good decisions in my life. I will form this board of directors with people who radiate the qualities I seek to create in my life. Today, I will pick up the phone and call a mentor, an advocate, or a teacher to seek wisdom and guidance in my life. One day, I want to be on the board of directors for someone, so I will begin living with wisdom daily.

3. *Today*, I will seek and accept feedback as feed forward. I will not associate the people with the words and will only seek to listen with intent to improve. Today, I will see adversity as my greatest teacher and will value the negative things that happen in life. Today, I will seek not to judge others or assume motive, but rather listen with my head and my heart to improve. The fact that I listen with intent to improve will build credibility with others and will only grow my influence. Today, I will ask, "What can I do to help you," and "What can I do to improve." When I receive this feed forward I will not

judge or punish the messenger, only thank them for the message. I have the power to choose what I do with the information I gather.

4. *Today*, I will find and listen to as many smart people as I can. Today, I will go to the bookstore and buy that book I am interested in. Today, I will pick up the phone and call that individual who has the wisdom I am seeking. Today, I will plan to go to that seminar I've been discussing. Today, I will see the day as a learning laboratory to glean as much information as I can. Today, I will create the action plan to continue my education in some capacity. Today, I will quit denying that knowledge gives me options and will seek that knowledge.

5. *Today*, I will become humble and teachable. Today, I will fully comprehend that I do not want to fall victim to atrophy. Today, I will fully grasp that the mind's need is to learn and expand and I can only do that when I become humble and teachable. Today, I will check my pride and ego at the door and become a sponge to the teaching of others. I will allow information and knowledge to inspire and uplift me. Today, I will grow my knowledge by realizing the first step on the path to education is to admit my ignorance. Today, I will model learning to all I associate with and will not attach formal titles to my assumptions of others knowledge bases.

Today, I will learn from everyone, including children and peers.

6. *Today*, I will view my workday as a "learning experience." Today, I will approach life and my job as an adventure that is fun and exciting. Today, I will open my mind and my heart to possibility. I will dream and hope again and believe again. Today, I will even learn from the mistakes of others to be sure not to repeat those mistakes. Today, I have decided to become a lifelong learner and will use every experience to only sharpen my skills to be effective.

7. *Today*, I will listen to my internal compass as it relates to my vocation. I will fully understand the difference between an occupation and a vocation. I will no longer see my job as a means to a financial end, but rather as an opportunity to connect to my source, contribute meaning to the world, and effectively leave a legacy to those with whom I associate. Today, I will seek to detect my voice if I have not found it and share it with others if I have. Today, I will make a significant difference in the world. Today, I will be a "creative force" in the world.

# Chapter 5 - Pay Up

## Key No. 5 Unlocks the Door to the Process of Manifestation and Using Adversity to Accelerate Progress

*Seven Processes to Get Where You Are Going*

In today's society many people simply do not want to pay the price or build the capacity to reach a goal. They spend valuable time and energy talking about what they want to do but seldom act on those conversations. As a matter of fact, I tell people when I'm speaking that the word *goal* is one of the most overused and underdone things in America. Think about your own life. When was the last time you took the time and energy to think (vision) about where you are and where you want to go (discipline). Stopping to think alone is more than most Americans ever attempt. To go somewhere you must reflect on where you are, and this takes pausing in life to study, investigate, feel, think, understand the true context of your current situation, and accept it as it is. Many people begin the year with a New Year's Resolution and decide that day to change it because it is just too hard or because of some other perceived roadblock. Think about this as it relates to goals. The term January derives from the Greek Goddess Janus who had two faces, one that looks backward to reflect on the past, and one that looks forward to focus on the future; hence the term January, or new beginning. In the beginning people want to change, reach a new level of success, or become somewhat inspired to create prosperity in life only to have the gravitational pull of society to pull them back down.

My point is simple. Study where you currently are. Think about where you want to go. Create an action plan for getting there. Act on that thought. Reflect on the results and then adjust accordingly. By using this key you begin to understand that there is a process to achievement and significance and that process cannot be denied. You also understand that there will be adversities along the way and how you view those adversities and use them to your benefit will either drive or prohibit your significance in life.

In this chapter, I'll outline seven key principles and processes that you must go through and experience to reach that level of success you've been talking about. Remember this—vision without execution is only hallucination.

# 1. Realize Everyday at Your Current Job Is an Interview for Your Next Job

At 18 years old I went back to the elementary school I attended and told the principal I wanted to coach basketball. He looked at me and said it could never happen. I was adamant about my passion for the game and finally convinced him I was worthy. He put me with an adult and we co-coached that team to a state championship in our first year and a state runner-up in year two. *That one decision was a defining moment in my life.* I used the very concepts I have discussed in this book– wake up, dream up, clean up, listen up, pay up, build up, act up–to continue to climb the ladder to where I am today. That decision was important because I understood the concept, "Everyday at your current job is an interview for you next job." When I was coaching that elementary team I wore a suit and treated every day like I was in the big time. That led to my next assignment as an assistant at one of the largest high schools in Tennessee at the age of 19. I was named the head freshman coach while I was in college and used that time (19–21) to grow my influence with everyone at the school and earn my keep. That led to me taking over as the head coach of the women's program at 22 when I was named the youngest head coach in the state of Tennessee. I have been there eleven years now and just assumed the responsibilities of athletic director. I look forward to serving the coaches and using the principles outlined in this book to take the program to the next level.

My point here is simple. If you approach your current job as an interview for your next job, you will work everyday with a passion, purpose, and focused intention toward improvement. When you do this, people notice, you grow your influence and begin to move up in the world. Many people stagnate in their jobs and become complacent and then complain to others that they are unhappy and they cannot move up in the company. You've got to work at the outside edge of your influence by taking initiative on your own to grow these things. Too many people just sit and wait for something to happen to them. You have to make things happen, and the first step toward doing that is to think there is ALWAYS something bigger out there for you than where you currently are. Practice Key No. 2 and begin to DREAM UP!

# 2. Understand There Is No Shortcutting the Process to Success—The Law of the Harvest Always Wins

I use this illustration all the time during my lectures. I ask the audience if it is possible to get both a high school and college diploma and still not be educated. The common response is yes. You can cheat your way through both situations and still not be educated. But you really did not cheat the process, did you? You really are not educated because you do not have the knowledge to be successful in the world. The law of the harvest factors into everything as it relates to success. Farmers understand this better than anyone. When you plant seeds, they must be gardened with proper sunlight, water, and tending to over a period of time. Without these simple things the harvest will not come to bear a crop. Success is exactly the same way. What you sow is what you will reap and you must pay the price and go through the process to become successful. Too many people in today's society go for the wealth without work approach to success. This is an illusion. The going rate for any worthwhile win in today's society is ten good setbacks. That means you may fail ten times before you really get where you are going. The only real difference between successful people and other folks is that some fall out of contention after only a few failures.

If you understand this concept you approach failure as learning opportunities and stepping stones to future successes. If you try to cheat the process you may reach some level of success but will most likely fall short of true significance which is what I think most of us are living for. Understand there will be many setbacks on the road to success and the price must be paid and the process must be followed. Natural principles govern our world so what you put in you will most likely get in return. This applies to both human relationships and your work. Have you ever tried to quick fix an important relationship with some technique or strategy? Most likely the other person saw right through that façade and you actually destroyed trust versus building it. Begin today by not trying to shortcut your way to the top. Value your time at the bottom or middle of the ladder of success. It will help you to better understand how to help those people when you get in a position of influence and you will only reach a level of influence if you understand the law of the harvest.

# 3. You Have to "Garden the Garden"

This is self-explanatory and common sense. *Unfortunately, common sense is not always common practice.* To continue the climb in your life you must constantly tend to your garden. This applies to sharpening your skills, continuing to grow and expand, and challenging the process along the way. Let's take the first concept of sharpening your skills. Here are some key concepts to gardening your garden along the journey to the top.

1. Take care of your four dimensions:
   a. Body - Exercise regularly and always present yourself in a professional manner
   b. Mind - Sharpen your mind by becoming a continual learner.

    c. Heart - Mend the relationships in your life that are strained and begin practicing non-judgment of others

    d. Spirit - Connect to meaningful projects in your life where you can pour you heart and soul

2. Continue to grow and expand and challenge the process.

    a. Challenge the current ways you think and see things by asking why you believe the way you do.

    b. Complete a life inventory to see where you are and where you are going.

    c. Listen (with an open mind and open heart) to concepts and ideas that are in direct contrast to you.

    d. Become humble and teachable and realize that you do not know everything.

As you continue to "garden your garden" you will be making yourself marketable to the rest of the world because you will be a hot commodity and seen as an asset to any organization and a solution to the problems that many industries face. The marketplace needs people who are solutions oriented, not problem oriented. Seek to become the answers to the problems versus contributing to the problems, and watch your stock rise. Once you obtain the job you want, think in terms of what you can do for the company versus what the company can do for you and you will begin to expand your influence.

# 4. Realize the Climb to the Top Will Be Filled with Many Rises

## *(Now You Can See More Than You Ever Have Before)*

When Stephen Covey began to write the best seller *The 8th Habit,* he said in the acknowledgements that because of a lifetime of teaching leadership and organizational effectiveness he thought it would only take six months to write the book. He stated that one of the great learnings of his life was if you wanted to make a new contribution, you have to make a whole new preparation *(See Key No. 1–Wake Up)*. To go beyond the past you must cultivate a new paradigm, a new perspective. After a year of teaching material and writing, Covey and his team finished a rough draft and they were thrilled they finally had arrived. Covey said, "It was at that moment we experienced what hikers often discover when climbing mountains. We hadn't reached the summit at all, only the top of the first rise." From that vantage point they could see things they had never seen before in ways they had never thought before. Covey went through that process of getting to a new rise nearly a dozen times until they finally reached the summit and finished the book five years later. I can identify with this climb. I initially began writing this book over three years ago and spoke on many of the concepts in over eighty speaking engagements around the world until finally I found the keys I was looking for. Those keys were what I referred to at the time as "the seven principles of success." I was convinced that they offered the framework I was searching for to complete this book. Then finally on a vacation to Alaska, I found just what I was looking for—time and inspiration.

As you climb the ladder of success many times you will feel like through all of your hard work and commitment that you are there. At that point you too will be at a rise where you can see new things that you could never see before. Truthfully, I don't know if we ever get to the top but each rise is very rewarding and in the end it's the climb that will be the most memorable. Cherish those rises and continue to climb that mountain.

# 5. Sharpen Your Perception through Investigation

In life you need a healthy, investigative awareness about what is working and what is not. Many people unfortunately develop a functional blindness to their own defects and shortcomings and never fully sharpen their perception through investigation into whether their strategies are working or not. This is the part of the book that I'm going to ask you the infamous question that Dr. Phil asks his guests, "How is it working for you?" I have seen too many people continue to do things for years that never work. I have seen people stay in jobs, in relationships, in misery for years because of two things: the inability to confront the brutal facts and their inability to act on what they know. Tara Bennett-Goleman (2001) wrote in *Emotional Alchemy*, "If we see only through the lens of our assumptions—our thoughts and beliefs—we are not in touch with how these lenses distort the reality of the moment." By constantly analyzing all parts of your life through this sharpening of your investigative skills you are completing the cycle of *The Belief and Action Model* mentioned at the beginning of the book. The cycle ends with reflection on what is working and not working in your life and begins again and is never ending with believing that you can change what is not working.

Begin to study your life, both personal and professional with intent to learn, grow, and become challenged by the process so you can become better. Remember from earlier readings, accept feedback as a gift that will help you reach the next level in your life. Many times, in my lectures I call this "completing an autopsy." I borrowed the terminology from Jim Collins in *Good to Great*. As you complete autopsies on your life of both the good and the bad you create an environment in your head and in your heart where the truth can be heard and not filtered. This gives you an accurate barometer and gauge to work with for future decisions. It is only after we are willing to reflect on the actuality of our life can we accept situations as they are and make the necessary improvements for the future.

# 6. Use Adversity to Accelerate Progress

In the very beginning of this book I mentioned that there were several common themes that I found from people in all walks of life as I have traveled the country. The first was the gap between thinking and doing or what I refer to as the execution gap. This is a commonality among most organizations as well. The second common theme is that *ALL people and ALL organizations* will face some level of adversity in their lives. We do not know what level of adversity that will be, but we can rest assured that it will be there. How can we spur people to act on what they think versus merely converse about? And the second question is how can we use adversity in our lives to accelerate progress in life instead of little or no movement toward taking positive action?

Last year, in the middle of our basketball season three of my better players were injured. All the people following our program believed we were finished, but not me. I sat down with my staff and said we have to come up with a way to use this adversity to our benefit. We completed a five-point plan for using adversity to accelerate progress, and I have been teaching that plan ever since. It is outlined in the next subheading. The point here is a big one. If we know that unfortunate things are going to happen to all of us, don't you think it would be wise to decide today that we are going to use those things to our benefit versus our detriment? This simple concept will become very powerful in your life as you meet challenges and will most likely separate the contenders from the pretenders. Life really is about one degree of separation from others, especially in competitive markets. By using perceived bad things in life to produce good things, you may very well be on your way to creating that separation between you and your competitors.

# 7. Create a Five-Point Plan for Using Adversity to Make You Better

When you have a plan you are prepared to meet the unexpected. Knowing that we live in a permanent whitewater society where the only constant is change, I feel it is very important to have a mindset, a paradigm, a plan to meet that sea of change. This plan will help you create a mental model to go through every time something bad happens to you in your life and will most certainly help you view those negative things as learning experiences. I have taught this plan to people in all walks of life all across America. It has universal meaning and applicability. Here are the steps:

1. Replace the question, "Why is this happening to me or us?" with "What is this trying to teach me or us?"
2. Decide from the beginning that no one will become reactive and blame outside circumstances for what happened. It simply is what it is. Complaining or blaming

will only make you part of the problem versus part of the solution.

3. Complete an autopsy of the situation without blaming anyone and decide that **YOU will** overcome this challenge.
4. Maximize the resources you have and work with a passion and focus to overcome the challenge. Many times a crisis is exactly what people need to wake up and confront the brutal facts about their lives.
5. Form a plan and ACT! Proactive people use adversity to prosper. It is that simple.

As mentioned earlier, the Organization of Victimization did a study of people who had some serious adversity in their lives including cancer patients, prisoners of war, and traumatic car accidents to see how they responded. They found the following findings:

1. The first group of people was permanently dispirited by the adversity. They never got back to normal.
2. The second group got back to normal but that was it.
3. The third group used the event as a defining moment in their lives to become even better than where they were before the event happened.

When adversity hits you which group will you fall into? Keep in mind, between every stimulus in life that you have you and your response to that stimulus you have a space. In that space lies your ability to choose your response. When you understand this concept you realize that in the end you actually begin to create the stimuli with your response to it. By using adversity to accelerate progress in your life there are no bad experiences, only learning experiences. If you take this approach there is also no failure, only experience. This simple concept will go very far in helping you live a life of deep meaning and significant contribution because you will value EACH *step of the process*. There will be no bad days, only good days filled with learning and growth en route toward a destination.

# Chapter 5 Summary— Seven Action Items to Manifest the Key Pay Up

1. *Today*, I will work with intent, purpose, presence, and passion at my current job because I know that I have an opportunity to build advocates and make a difference. Today, I will fully understand that I am not where I need to be on the way to getting there. Today, I will evaluate my current situation and will work to improve it. Today, I will understand that I am a solution to the challenges we face in the workplace and I will work to grow my influence with others and improve their perceptions

of me. Today, I will serve human needs in principle-centered ways.

2. *Today*, I will fully understand that there are natural laws and principles that govern life. I will understand that there is no quick way to become successful and that every worthwhile goal I plan to achieve will take time, patience, persistence, and perseverance. Today, I will work to sow good things which I will tend daily with a singleness of purpose toward my destination. Today, I will become the change I seek to create in the world by matching up internal thoughts with external action. Today, I will pay the price to be successful.

3. *Today*, I will "garden my garden." Today, I will decide what the most important things in my life are and will invest my time and energy in alignment with those things. Today, I will understand that true achievement and significance begins with the seed of a dream and belief and only manifests by connecting to source and working diligently in the direction of those dreams. Today, I will cultivate the discipline to act daily around my highest priorities and will focus on execution.

4. *Today*, I will stop and take a moment to view where I currently stand in life and where I want to go. I will work with fervor to climb the mountain of success realizing I may never get there but that each rise will help me see

life in new and exciting ways. Today, I will value where I am but will not be satisfied with staying here. Today, I will pack the tools I need to climb the mountain and will focus on placing the right tools in my luggage. Today, I will learn new skills to take with me along the journey and will not discount anyone else's ideas because I may be able to use them in the future.

5. *Today*, I will investigate my current way of thinking and living and see where I am aligned with my conscience. Today, I will realize that the pressures of life and the win-lose society we live in will work to only hinder and hold me back from realizing my potential if I allow it to. Today, I will sharpen my perception of the world in which I operate and will seek first the benefit of those around me, versus my own benefit. Today, I will become a continual evaluator of my life and how my actions affect others. Today, I will enter the college of studying my thoughts, my tendencies, and my actions.

6. *Today*, I will value adversity. Today, I will understand that adversity can become an event that causes me to study current ways of thinking and doing that are unproductive. Today, I will understand that adversity can make me stronger, make me value things I have neglected, and make me express my love for others. Today, I will not need adversity to teach me that I should be thankful for my current situation and for the people

in my life. Today, I will use ANY adversity to accelerate progress versus little or no movement. Today, I will be thankful that adversity has taught me some of the most valuable lessons of my life.

7. *Today*, I will create a plan to use perceived negative experiences in my life for benefit versus harm. Today, I will understand that the key to successful living is through wisdom and I can only gather wisdom through experience. Today, I will use the very adversity that paralyzes some to create improvement in my life. Today, I will value adversity.

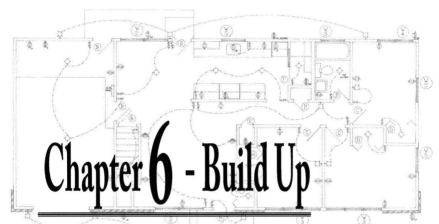

# Chapter 6 - Build Up

## Key No. 6 Unlocks the Door to Synergy, Belief in Others, and Creative Cooperation
### *Seven Opportunities for Synergy*

As we begin to grow and mature we come to understand some simple principles. The rent we pay for living on this earth is paid in our service to others. As we climb the emotional ladder we also comprehend that the best way to achieve significant, sustainable significance in life is by losing ourselves in service to others. Lately, I have personally come to realize that a great life is one that is built around "living inspired" and trying to achieve an "everyday greatness." One common theme that continues to resurface in my life is that of being true to principle and not allowing the negative undertone of the world or scarcity minded people to control my hopes or dreams.

This sixth principle is built around an abundant paradigm that teaches us that there is enough out there in the world for us to have all we want without ever having to take away from another or being jealous of the success of another. This is in stark contrast to the prevalent mindset of most people who are deeply rooted in win-lose thinking, becoming almost obsessed with confessing the sins of others, and making excuses or rational on why they do not have a bigger piece of the pie. This key teaches us that if you really want to be successful, you help other people be successful. A nice habit to cultivate as it relates to practicing this key is to constantly search for opportunities to build others up versus tear others down. Practice tolerance for other people's views and opinions, and do not become easily offended if those views are not in alignment with yours. Listen with intent to understand versus intent to reply and truly seek the benefit of others first versus your own benefit. In essence, BUILD and think in terms of service and contribution back to the greater good. In the process a funny thing will happen, others will return to you what you project to the world. Begin today by BUILDING UP!

# 1. Believe in Abundance vs. Scarcity

As you move from interdependent thinking into the interdependent realities of the world you begin to realize that the only way to true significance is by "co-missioning" with others. It is through synergy and the combination of talents that we negate our weaknesses and build on both our strengths and the strengths of others toward our destination. To do this effectively we must learn to think in ways of abundance versus scarcity. Let me illustrate the two paradigms.

*Scarcity mentality* thinking stems from a paradigm of control and fear where one believes that in order to succeed in life she must do so at the expense of others. This person believes that there is only one pie and if others get a piece then there will not be any left for her. This person has hidden agendas and is into undermining, backstabbing, pulling down, comparing, contending, criticizing, competing, and politicking. This is not a category you want to be in but one most people live in unfortunately. This negative cycle begins at an early age and becomes apparent later in life. If you don't believe me, just go and watch a pee-wee football, basketball, or baseball game. The parents focus on the benefit of one, their child, versus the benefit of all. This type of thinking continues to build an individualistic paradigm around competing with others for a sense of self-worth and potential. A strong sense of self-awareness is needed to overcome this type of negative thinking and become genuinely happy for the successes of the group. Life is interdependent, not independent, period. The faster we teach young people this through modeling the more tolerance we will build, the more unity we will build, and the more fulfillment we will build.

*Abundance mentality* thinking stems from a paradigm of abundance and infinite possibilities and unlimited opportunity. This person believes that there is enough success and happiness out there for everyone to have all they want and they never have to compete, criticize, or compare his self to others. This person believes in the potential and worth of others and is sincerely happy for the success of others. This person also understands the concept, "If you want to retain those who are present, be loyal to those who are absent." Therefore, he does not speak negatively or enable the badmouthing of others when they are not present. This is where most people want to live but allow circumstances, the environment, or the gravitational pull of an individualistic society to pull them into scarcity thinking.

As you can see it is clear which mindset you should live from. If it is that easy then why do so many people operate from a scarcity mindset? That answer is fairly simple to me. We live in such a competitive win-lose society that we are taught from an early age that we must compare ourselves with the material things of others, we must step over to get ahead, and we must climb the ladder of success at all cost. The real key to achievement, to significance is through others. Study history and all major success stories of moral authority and you will find that only through the movement of a group of people did anything large ever get accomplished. One person might have been the change catalyst to start the movement, but others have to be enlisted to make the major contributions.

This brings me back to a point I made earlier in the book, that of a trim-tabber. A trim-tab is the small rudder on the big rudder of a plane or ship that turns the whole plane or ship. This small piece, when it moves, moves the big piece that in turn moves the entire thing. A person of great influence can be a trim-tabber, someone who with one movement moves the whole organization or possibly even a whole civilization. Keep in mind, "Nothing happens until something moves." You be the person that takes the initiative to move in the direction of significance. If you want to achieve everyday greatness, stop being so concerned about who will get the credit and ante up what you can bring to the team.

# 2. Search for Teachable Opportunities

In life there are opportunities, opportunities to share one's knowledge, skills, and soul with others. As we begin to move up the ladder of interdependence and fully understand this concept of building others up, we search for those opportunities to share with others. I noted earlier in the book about developing your gift and giving that gift away to as many people as you can. In essence that is exactly what I am doing by speaking and writing, but this comes in a variety of forms for people everywhere. It could be a crucial conversation with a friend, a family member, a constituent, a co-worker, or simply a stranger. As a coach and athletic director, I search for opportunities to connect my voice (calling in life) with a touch during a conversation with others. I am constantly searching for the right opportunity to convey my appreciation and affirm and validate the worth and potential in others in so clearly a way they begin to see it in themselves. Sometimes the best conversations are ones where there is no talking at all, only silent communication, where feelings are so strong that you can feel the other person expressing love, disappointment, hurt, or anger.

These crucial conversations will put enormous deposits into the emotional bank accounts of others and will build the trust account in ways that are immeasurable. The people we associate with the most have to be affirmed the most because the expectations of the relationship are so much higher. Begin today to search for opportunities to build others up versus participate in the negativity and reactiveness of tearing others down. This will lead to meaning and satisfaction at the end of the day versus a profound misalignment with your conscience. When you participate in the negativity that is so pervasive in the world today you become part of the problems of society versus part of the solution and this creates an inner animosity with your soul that will ultimately lead to unhappiness.

# 3. Communicate and Validate the Worth and Potential of Others

To reach any level of success there must be a constant, continual, repetitive reenforcement of that belief. You must continue to confirm, validate, appreciate, and inspire those around you, beginning with yourself. Remember, those who we associate with the most need the most deposits. As we reaffirm the potential and worth in others, we are expressing our voices and inspiring others to find their voices in the process. To revisit an earlier concept in the book you express your voice in four unique ways:

1. Vision - You see a better world for you and your group through the mind's eye.
2. Discipline - You become a disciple to other people and the cause you deem worthy. You affirm that belief an discipline to others.
3. Passion - You have the inner drive and intrinsic motivation to complete the journey with fire and enthusiasm.
4. Conscience - You move in the direction of your dreams and are guided by a deep conscience or need and longing to live a life of significance.

Notice how this repetitive cycle focuses on the whole person of your four dimensions of:

1. Vision - Mind
2. Discipline - Body
3. Passion - Heart
4. Conscience - Spirit

By the expression of your voice to others you embark upon a journey toward significance, and you have the road map to complete the mission. As you live out of your imagination and attach your actions with integrity (which means living an integrated life around principles in the totality of your life) you work in principle-centered ways which produces an alignment with your inner core or spirit. This will lead to more happiness and fulfillment both in your personal and professional life. Continue to reinforce your beliefs with both your actions and your words so that others see you as legitimate and sincere about your efforts.

# 4. Build Yourself First from All Four Dimensions

To build others up you must first get to a place in your own life so that you have the capacity to help others. You must first find your unique voice before you can inspire others to find theirs. To do this you need a holistic approach to developing four capacities or four intelligences that derive from your four dimensions noted in the book. You must build

1. IQ - Intelligent Quotient (Mind)
2. EQ - Emotional Intelligence (Heart)
3. PQ - Physical Intelligence (Body)
4. SQ - Spiritual Intelligence (Spirit)

Remember the four needs of the complete person:

1. To live (body)
2. To learn (mind)
3. To love (heart)
4. To leave a legacy (spirit)

As you understand this you begin to build capacity in all areas making you a well-rounded, complete person who has the intelligences to compete in a global economy. In essence, you become a commodity to the world yourself because of your knowledge, skills, desire, and beliefs. So many of the people that I speak to around the country are simply unhappy and feel that they have so much more to give in both their personal and professional lives. They are frustrated (misguided enthusiasm) and intimidated and are searching for answers to live an integrated life. This model or framework of the whole person gives a complete picture from which to work. When all four of these dimensions are clicking in a profession you are well on your way to doing what you love and loving what you do which is in direct contrast to upward of 70 percent of most Americans who do not enjoy their professional careers and are unhappy with their personal lives.

Here are a few suggestions for developing the four capacities to meet the realities of the knowledge worker era:

1. For the mind - Read, grow, expand, challenge yourself in multi-dimensions
2. For the heart - Mend relationships, see the good in others, affirm the potential in others, and build up other versus tear down. Practice abundance versus scarcity.
3. For the body - Practice consistent, repetitive exercise. Eat healthy and value yourself.
4. For the Spirit - Connect to your inner core, find a cause to believe in, lose yourself in service to others, and practice a weekly or daily spirituality.

Once you cultivate and build the internal discipline to these four intelligences you will grow your influence with yourself and grow your influence with others. Have you ever seen someone who tried to lead when they themselves were flawed with duplicity, poor character, inability to make and keep commitments, or were a physical mess? The internal strength you build will carry over and flow into all areas of your life making you an integrated person.

# 5. Practice Building Up Daily: Great Leaders Make Others Believe They Are Better Than What They Are

I am a firm believer that good leaders affirm the worth and potential in others in so clearly a way that they pull the best out. Think about your own life. Were there not people who separated your conditions or poor attitudes from your future potential and communicated that to you? They believed in the good of you when it was easy to see the bad. They, in essence, helped you find your voice. I think back to one of my first speaking engagements when that gentleman named David Forrest walked up to me and said I should go on the circuit because of my talents. I think back to Marc LaBlanc, who at an Achiever's Circle in 2003 told me I should write my first book. At that time, they saw something in me that I did not see, and that affirmation kick started the process of discovering my voice. Those two instances took place in a single day. They were transformational. As you interact with others, you begin to see their potential and validate and communicate that potential to them. I am afforded the opportunity all the time as a coach and speaker but you can find endless opportunities to build up the confidence of others in your daily interactions with all those you associate.

I like to tell one of my favorite stories about a blind horse named Dusty. It illustrates the power of building people up to make them believe they are better than what they really are.

You see, I was driving in the country of my hometown of Woodbury, Tenn., when I accidentally ran off the road. Cell phones do not work in that part of the country (can you hear me now? NO!), so I had only one choice and that was to ask a stranger up the road to help me out. He had a barn out back and said he only had one blind horse named Dusty, but we could hook Dusty up to the car and try and pull it out. Desperate and out of options I took the offer. After we hooked Dusty up he said, "Pull Star, pull." Dusty didn't move. He yelled out, "Pull Charlie, pull." Dusty just stayed put and I'm thinking that this guy is crazy and possibly psychotic. The third time he said, "Pull Dallas, pull." Again, Dusty didn't move. The fourth time he yelled, "Pull Dusty, pull." With a mighty heave and a ho Dusty pulled my vehicle out. I was excited but also confused. I told the gentleman, "I really appreciate the help, but I don't quite understand. You called three different horse's names out before Dusty's. What was that about?" He said, "Are you kidding, Dusty is blind, not deaf. If he thought he had to do all that work by himself he would have never tried it." I laughed but definitely got the point, and you should to. Sometimes you have to make others believe they have four horsepower when they only have one. Limiting yourself in your own mind will get you absolutely nowhere. How will other people believe in you and your abilities if you don't believe in yourself? Identify those roadblocks in your mind today and start acting like the person you want to be vs. the one you have always been. *Sometimes the way you see the problem is the problem.* Regardless of the way you have been scripted by your parents (genetic determinism) you can effectively become a transition person, one that goes beyond past limitations and boundaries and changes the situation for the future. *Never let your past hold your future hostage, never.*

# 6. Don't Participate in the Negativity

In life you always have a choice about what you participate in. Anyone can certainly be negative at any time but you need to ask yourself this question before you do: What has going negative ever gotten you? In my own life going negative has either left me embarrassed or ashamed and usually put me in a lose-lose situation. As it relates to building others up and illuminating the good in others there is simply no room for going negative. I believe that each of us has a certain amount of energy for the day. We get to decide where we place and how we use that energy. We can make a conscious choice to participate in areas that drain our energy or pit us in power struggles that result in broken relationships that may never heal. When I first started coaching at the age of fifteen I thought I had to go negative when I became intense. The behavior was usually rewarded by results of winning so I really believed that it worked. Then I became educated. Just two years ago a good friend of mine named Randy Coffman taught me a valuable lesson—you can remain positive *and* still be intense. I call it the value of "and."

Many times in life we simply see things in black and white. We cannot see the two sides, only one side which leaves us locked in a creativity prison based on our past scripting. If you can begin to embrace the power of "and" you can see that you can have two opposing things at once if you just open your mind and choose to see it. I try my best not to participate in the negativity that only stifles growth and builds division among people. If we can just embrace the fact that others can be successful too, we can actually be happy for their successes versus jealous of what they have to offer. Remember, jealously stems from a paradigm of fear and insecurity and manifests itself in terms of pulling others down, backstabbing, or of all things, going negative. If you really want to maximize the potential you have start by understanding that we are all one group of people traveling down the same journey in search of the same thing, meaning. Choose today not to participate in the negativity and to become a light that illuminates the good in others. It will be one of the best decisions you will ever make.

# 7. Practice Three Key Habits to Unleash Creative Cooperation

When you build others up you seek their benefit first before your own benefit. Through the power of intention this will most likely attract back into your life the flow of positive energy from others that also see the good in you. In tense situations where emotions are high and people believe strongly one thing or another, I have found it useful to practice three key habits of synergy, as first introduced to me by my favorite author, Dr. Stephen Covey.

**Habit-** *Think in terms of Win-Win vs. Win-Lose.* Search for alternatives where each person wins.

**Habit-** *Seek first the benefit of others versus your own benefit.* Truly listen and feel with a sincere intent to walk in the shoes of another. Detach yourself from your current role and view life through the lens of another. I call this "paradigm trading" where you really try to see things from their perspective.

**Habit-** *Search for third alternatives.* Too many times in life we simply think in win-lose mindsets. This is a natural manifestation from all of the competition based identities we are scripted and shaped with as children. Go to the table with an open mind and an open heart and practice each one of these key habits and chances are you WILL find a solution to the challenge you are facing.

# Chapter 6 Summary— Seven Action Items to Manifest the Key Build Up

1. *Today*, I will believe and act in abundance versus scarcity. Today, just as the universe and the air are infinite and abundant, so too will my possibilities become infinite and abundant. Today, I will live inspired and be inspirational to others because I will seek to build up versus tear down. Today, I will become aware of my insecurities and jealousies and seek to transform them into confidence, belief, and hope for others. Today, I will begin to build people up in my daily interactions with others and will not waste precious energy on negative people.

2. *Today*, I will search for teachable opportunities with others. I will realize that others will become open, humble, and vulnerable to me when I become open, humble, and vulnerable to them. Today, I will view life as an upward spiral of learning and growing and will approach each day with an intent to grow my knowledge, skills, desire, and belief. Today, I will search to find my voice and once found, I will seek to inspire others to find their voices. Today, I will value those crucial

conversations I have with others and will grasp the golden opportunities to impart wisdom on others.

3. *Today,* I will reinforce belief in myself and in others. Today, I will understand that confidence is the memory of success and success can only be achieved through consistent, repetitive practice. Today, I will affirm and validate the worth and potential in myself and in others. I will seek to match my internal thoughts with my external actions. Today, I will see people for what they could become versus what they are. Today, I will not judge, compare, criticize, complain, contend, or fall victim to complacency on my journey of improvement. Today, I will illuminate the positive in others versus the negative.

4. *Today,* I will understand that a whole person is made up of four parts: body, mind, heart, and spirit. I will understand that to build another up by using this whole person paradigm that I will have to pay them fairly (for the body), use them creatively (for the mind), treat them kindly (for the heart), and help them connect to meaning and source (for the spirit). Today, I will not neglect one dimension but will see the complete picture and will use the whole person paradigm as an accurate source to diagnose and predict the challenges we face in the world. Today, I will understand that each of these four parts produces four unique needs: to live (for the body), to

learn (for the mind), to love (for the heart), and to leave a legacy (for the spirit). Once I grasp this concept, I will better utilize my voice in helping others find their voices.

5. *Today*, I will seek to build others up and treat them solely from a perspective of their potential versus their weakness. Today, I will help people believe and dream again. Today, I will offer hope through affirmation, validation, appreciation, and motivation and will not use fear, power, or position to get another to move in a certain direction.

6. *Today*, I will choose not to participate in any negativity. Today, I will defend those who are not present or will walk away from negative people who only seek the benefit of themselves at the expense of another. Today, I will choose to operate from a perspective of positive energy and goodness versus negative energy and wasted time. Today, I will not allow others to define who I am or where I am going. Today, I will not be concerned with social status but rather with aligning my life with correct principles that benefit the greater good. Today, I will remain positive even as life challenges me.

7. *Today*, I will seek the benefit of others first versus my own benefit. Today, I will seek to trade paradigms with another versus judge, criticize, or downgrade. Today, I will search for third alternatives to challenges versus

become emotional and stuck in old, outdated ways of finding answers that rely on formal position. Today, I will think outside the box versus remain stagnant and still. Today, I will be dynamic and will seek to become the change I wish to see in the world.

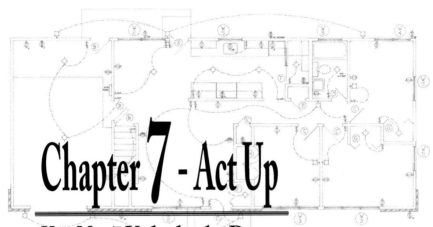

# Chapter 7 - Act Up

## Key No. 7 Unlocks the Door to Execution and Completion

*Seven Core Drivers to Success*

The process of this book has been a long and exhilarating journey. Today, I chose to take up space at a local lake in Nashville, Tenn., to finish work on the final works of Chapter Seven which centers on possibly the most important concept of the book, action. As I sit at a park bench and overlook Percy Priest Lake, I am overwhelmed with emotion and passion. Just yesterday I spoke at a men's breakfast and shared with a small group how I truly believe that by practicing these seven, simple keys of life that one can live inspired daily, make a significant contribution to the greater good, and live a life of deep meaning and passionate execution.

Easily the largest execution gap in America is that of an inability to act, an inability to translate thought into action. For some reason, there are a variety of variables that affect people's ability to take a stimulus and turn it into reality. This problem is epidemic across the country and I think stems from an imbalance in the four dimensions of body, mind, heart, and spirit. For too long people have simply settled for a life of mediocrity and average accomplishments. We have a choice daily to become great. In our life, everyone has a choice, as Stephen Covey says, one road is the broad well-traveled road to mediocrity which straightjackets human potential and self-worth. The other road is the road less traveled, which is the road to greatness and meaning. For some strange reason we can create a better vision in our heads, but do not have the fortitude to make that thought part of who we are. As I have traveled around the country I have seen countless examples of people who so desperately want a better life. They are discouraged and distressed and are looking for something that can profoundly affect their lives. I believe that something can be found in simplicity. As you finish this challenge I encourage you to live daily, to learn continuously, to love abundantly, and to leave a legacy for all those that follow. The biggest person we need to lead everyday is ourselves.

# 1. Between Stimulus and Response YOU have a CHOICE

One of the most important concepts that a person can ever understand is the concept of stimulus and response. Between what happens to you and how you respond is a space. In that space lies your ability and power to choose your response. This space is also present between thinking and doing, and unfortunately this is where the largest gap in the world exists— the infamous execution gap. In *Key No. 2—Dream Up* I asked you to live out of your imagination instead of your memory and not to allow your past to hold your future hostage. That aspect is the first creation of taking something from unmanifest into manifest. The second creation is in the actual action, the doing. If you realize that you are ultimately responsible for the success or failure of your life between your stimulus and response you ACT. Projecting blame onto others, being a victim of circumstance or past scripting, or making excuses for not executing only causes you to lose the private battles of your life, handcuffing and stifling your own credibility with yourself and others. You simply have to grasp the concept that you always have a choice in how you respond and within that choice lies the seeds of fruition or merely concepts of discussion. I think it is important for you to visually see what that space might look like so you have an idea when you experience this process.

**Figure 4. Stimulus and Response**

As you can see between what happens to you or between you having a thought and manifesting that thought lies this space. Proactive people use this space wisely by cultivating the self-discipline and capacity to act. Unmotivated and reactive people simply breakdown during that space and cannot complete the thought or action. This leads to an enormous disconnect within one's conscience and is a major contributor to low trust levels with others. Remember this simple statement, "People believe what you do, not what you say." If you are having an inability to complete and act during this space it is most likely because you have not built the much needed capacity through making and keeping commitments to yourself first. The daily private victory will lead to increased public victory and an inward and outward confidence.

Victor Frankl (1997) in *Man's Search for Meaning* said that the last and most precious freedom that individuals have is the power and freedom to choose. While in a Nazi prison camp Frankl lost most everything he had except his ability to decide how he handled the adversity he was facing. From that experience he defined an individual's ability to choose as "our last human freedom." Once you begin to understand that between your stimulus (a thought from inside your head or an external event) and your response (action taken from that thought or as a result of that event) you have a choice. Proactive people always realize that in that space between stimulus and response they always, always have a choice. Reactive people lack the self-discipline and capacity to act between their thoughts and actions and allow others actions to define them in ways they do not like. Proactive people are the creative factors of their life and do not empower other's weaknesses to control them.

The space looks similar to this:

**Figure 5. Converting Thought Into Action**

As you begin to understand that you have the power to choose, you fully realize that you control how you respond in virtually any situation that will ever happen to you in your life. You are let out of prison by others who seek to define you by the social mirror, by status, money, house, clothes, by ability, or by comparing and competing for your own sense of self-worth with others. This is entirely liberating and emancipating and will help you take full responsibility for your moods, thoughts, and feelings and free you from becoming dependent on others for your internal happiness.

As situations happen to you in life that you are not comfortable with, you have the ability to suspend thought and action during this space until you have the knowledge, skills, desire, or beliefs that you need to act in ways that are congruent with your true mission, which is the ultimate goal. Translating your espoused or internal mission to the moments of your life will create a dynamic feeling inside you of congruence, meaning, and purpose. This will connect you to your spirit just as I have been throughout the writing of this book. Translating your mission to your moment looks like this:

**Figure 6. Building Capacity**

Building Capacity

Translating the Mission to the Moment

Mission    20 Emotional Push-ups    Moment

Capacity to Meet Challenges

The twenty emotional push-ups noted between your mission and your moment represent the emotional maturity and capacity needed to act to meet the challenges of your life. If you fail to cultivate the internal strength to meet the external challenges you simply will not be able to connect the mission to the moment leaving you frustrated and intimidated by life and what others throw your way. The most important concept to understand is that you have the capacity to meet these challenges once you move from a reactionary stance toward life to a proactive stance. Now you just need to build the important ingredient, capacity.

# 2. Building Capacity to ACT!

Understanding now that you have the power to make anything happen and the power to choose your response to virtually any situation, it is now necessary to understand how you build the internal self-discipline to convert thought into action. There are a variety of factors that prohibit individuals from conversion but some I've witnessed include

- Fear of failure
- Fear of embarrassment
- Activity traps of life
- Too difficult

- Entrenched in old ways of acting
- Deeply embedded in failure mindsets
- Too much work
- Culture won't permit change
- Fear of change
- Fear of uncertainty

If you have allowed any of the above excuses to permeate your life and prohibit you from acting on your mental thought processes, you have held yourself hostage in a self-contained prison. Deep within each one of us is a longing, a hunger for meaning and contribution, a need to find our voices in life and make a difference. In a recent study fear of not making a difference in life ranked even higher than a fear of death. Why then do we allow factors, that for the most part, we can control to lock us out of realizing our potential in this world? My answer is simple. The lack of self-discipline to connect our mission to the moments of our lives straightjackets our potential and pushes us into living a life of default versus a life of design. How do we build this capacity?

**Twenty Emotional Pushups**

Just as there is an Emotional Bank Account (Covey, 1989) with others where the currency is trust there is also an Emotional Bank Account for which we have to make deposits. This is where the private victories are won allowing us the capacity to convert thoughts into actions and win the public victories in the eyes of society. Let me suggest several ways to build capacity to meet the challenge of creating action around our thoughts:

- Make and keep commitments to yourself
- Set goals and objectives and attain them
- Educate and obey your conscience by living from principles
- Plan, execute, then reflect for improvement
- Translate your deep internal mission into an emotionally charged situation
- Forgive others who transgress against you
- Become a light that illuminates the good in others
- Be loyal to those who are absent
- Do not use formal authority to bully someone into having your way
- Seek first the benefit of others versus your own benefit
- Move away from justifying your point when others disagree
- Lose pride and EGO. Both will cause you to make very poor decisions.
- Practice non-judgment of others
- Reflect on your internal dialogue and change it to positive thoughts
- Do not assume motive when dealing with others
- Live in the present, plan for the future, learn from the past
- Plan and execute time to reflect, exercise, educate yourself, and plan

- Learn to build others up (including yourself) versus tear them down
- Believe and practice abundance

As you can see you build capacity mainly by doing. Confidence is the memory of success and you become successful by constant repetition. Only through consistent buildup of skills and knowledge do you garner the capacity to act in touch situations in your life. To get there you must first identify the things that are limiting this process. Many are emotional cancers that create such a stalemate in your life that you simply lack the needed energy to act.

How do you build capacity to act in your work, in physical training, with your children, or with various projects in your life? You practice, right? You can only build the capacity to act in your life through consistent, repetitive action and experience. This process begins with winning the private victories in your life. Just as I noted earlier in the book, you must win the private victory daily so you can win the public victory later. You build capacity to act by educating your mind and your heart, by constantly expanding your horizons, growing your knowledge and skills, and by growing your desire and your beliefs. This sequential, integrated process begins by growing in four dimensions as noted throughout the book:

1. **For the mind** - Grow your knowledge through expansion, challenge, reading, and sharing of knowledge and ideas

2. **For the body** - Grow your health through regular exercise, a healthy diet, proper rest, and maintaining and challenging yourself to grow stronger

3. **For the heart** - Grow your passion through participating in causes you believe deeply in, practicing non-judgment of others, forgiving those who have transgressed against you, loving, and by being passionate about your vocation

4. **For the spirit** - Grow your conscience by making and keeping commitments to yourself and others, practicing regular reflection and renewal, spending time with nature, expressing your voice through your job, cultivating and connecting to your source, and practicing living with an open heart and mind.

You grow your capacity to act just like you would grow your capacity to lift weights. Start with 20 emotional pushups by translating your mission to a trying moment in your life, verbalizing something with both courage and consideration (one sign of maturity), and by making and keeping a commitment you feel strongly about. As you grow this capacity you will begin to live in alignment with what matters most to you and this congruence will light a fire in you that others will notice. Now, we must identify the roadblocks that may impede you from finding that voice and building that capacity.

# 3. Identify the Roadblocks Preventing You from Acting

Allow me to begin this section by outlining six emotional cancers. Five of the six I borrowed from Stephen Covey, but the sixth is one I added. First it is important to outline what cancer is. As noted in Peter Senge's (2004) book *Presence,* "A cell that loses its social identity reverts to blind undifferentiated cell division, which can ultimately threaten the life of the larger organism. It is what we know as cancer." Many people unfortunately have developed functional blind spots to the cancers that they have allowed to manifest in their lives therefore leading them to operate from an inaccurate and fragmented paradigm. Until they can "see" that they are emotionally connected or practice this cancerous behavior they just continue to wander aimlessly down life's path blaming and reacting to the short end of the stick they constantly subscribe to.

As I noted in the beginning of the book, you must stop and reflect on what is actually happening in your life and see if you are getting the results you really want. If not you could be affected by one of these six cancers.

- *Complaining-* A spirit of reactiveness that suggests that you have no control over your situation so you will just make everyone aware of your misery in an effort to manipulate them into massaging your heart. This is enormously unhelpful and wastes valuable energy toward trying to solve whatever it is you are experiencing. Ask yourself this question, "Has whining, pouting, moping, or blaming someone about a situation ever produced any positive outcomes?" If no, then simply stop.

- *Comparing* - When you compare yourself to others or the social mirror you are simply operating from a scarcity mindset. People are different for a reason and each person brings unique talents to the table. Getting into who is more popular, wears the nicest clothes, who is prettier, who lives in the biggest house, or who has the most money are reactive behaviors that robs us of our own uniqueness. The social mirror is a powerful script but a lousy one. Once you find your voice in life you won't be so concerned with social status but more attuned to what you are really doing with your life. Immature people compare themselves to others. Mature people value diversity and seek to see the beauty in all people, including their own.

- *Contending* - The concept of carrying a contentious spirit or negativity everywhere you go is highly reactive. You have one life. How you handle the daily challenges of that life determines your quality of life. Becoming negative, cynical, combative, or defensive makes you look back and produces a profound misalignment with your inner conscience. You will feel this misalignment and know deep down that you have more to offer the world than a negative spirit.

- *Criticizing* - Criticizing others stems from a view point of control, fear, insecurity, and scarcity. When we criticize others we look weak and it only promotes a dependence on the social mirror mentioned earlier. There's a reason we learned at an early age, "If you can't say something nice about someone, don't say anything at all." Think about it in all your conversations how others look when they criticize. Remember this very powerful statement, "If you want to retain those who are present, be loyal to those who are absent."

- *Competing* - When we compete internally against those we should be working with or against the social mirror for our own sense of self-worth, we simply lose. I certainly understand the value of competing having been a coach half of my life, but my basic belief is that cooperation will far exceed competition in the long run. I have been in situations in the workplace where everyone competed internally for support, value proposition, time, space, and certainly ego. These situations always led to lose-lose outcomes, and many times the individuals competing could not even see the wedge they used to supposedly win in the short term only to lose in the long term. This is a simple one. Value yourself and what you have to offer and value others around you. Cooperate internally and compete externally. Value your competition as your best teacher, not your worst enemy.

- *Complacency* - I added this emotional cancer to Covey's first five because I strongly believe that this one is an important killer to significance. The cancer of complacency assumes you have arrived and normally sets in when we become content with our current situation in life and have experienced some level of success. Many times I have personally witnessed individuals climb the ladder of success with passion, patience, persistence, and perseverance only to stagnate and plateau out and lose the very ferocity it took to get there. This is a very sad situation in all facets of life. Life is a journey filled with peaks and valleys and many times we only gain experience and knowledge by losing. We should constantly evaluate and reflect on what works and what does not and be on fire to learn and grow. Our unique human endowments of self-awareness and imagination allow us to constantly recreate ourselves in new and better ways and to grow daily as we experience new learning. Don't allow yourself to ever become complacent in life and just stay where you are. From my experiences complacency is entirely a reactive stance but usually stems from a disconnect from the source of passion or an event that dispirits the soul in such a way that you lose hope. This all stems from viewing people from the holistic perspective I've mentioned throughout this book. If you break someone's spirit hard enough, do not be surprised if they lose faith in the mission of the organization and withdraw into a state of complacency while they look for other people who value what they have to offer. The same is true in interpersonal relationships with others.

# 4. Start Small and Achievable

Unfortunately, in today's society many people want what they want when they want it, which is right now. Reflecting over my coaching and leadership career, I can see the small, incremental steps I took each step of the way to get where I am today. I can still remember coaching at a small elementary school in the beginning when I worked for $199.50 for two years. At that point in my life, it was the biggest thing I could be doing, and I understood the concept introduced earlier in the book, "Everyday at your current job is an interview for your future job." You see, people are always watching and observing and it's clear to see which individuals are driven by the expression of their voices through vision, discipline, passion, and conscience. The individuals who build an enormous reservoir of knowledge and talent in specific areas will eventually find and plug into an outlet and to the people they need to materialize their dreams.

There are a few important concepts to grasp when it comes to turning thought into action:

1. You must first understand the value of your time and how what you do affects the quality of your life as invested by the time you choose to expend.
2. You must understand that creating a vision for your life is one of the easiest parts. Many people talk a lot about what they could become.
3. You must learn to believe in your ability, cultivate a large knowledge base, and grow your capacity to act versus only converse.
4. Once you understand the power of the spirit and of conscience driving your actions when you have found your voice, there will be nothing that will stop you from achieving what you set out to do.
5. Goals are the most overused, underdone concept in America. Work from the four-dimensional approach to cultivate these capacities in the realization of your goals

    1. Mind- Vision- Imagination
    2. Body- Discipline- Execution
    3. Heart- Passion- Fuel
    4. Spirit- Conscience- Connection to Meaning

Once you find your voice at the intersection and balance these four intelligences and capacities, you will begin to live fully, love completely, learn daily, and seek to leave a legacy both in your organization and in your life. This will produce action around your vision. Remember, start small with daily private victories. It could include you practicing non-judgment today or simply going an entire day without being negative toward another. Small daily private victories will lead to large public victories. Where you are on the emotional maturity continuum will determine where you are and where you need to go.

# 5. Connect Your Mission to the Moment

Once you develop a mission that you believe in, emotionally identify with, and walk through the process of understanding stimulus and response, you are then ready to translate your mission to the tough moments of your life. This will allow you the power and freedom to act in ways that are deeply aligned with your inner voice and create actions around your highest priorities. Many people believe that mission statements are soft and mushy but the reality of the situation is that if used properly they become a powerful guiding force and constitution for your life. Most of the people that believe they do not work have not built the capacity to act; therefore, they put up defensive mechanisms allowing them to fail before they even get started. Please allow me to share my mission statement with you:

# PASSION PERSISTENCE PATIENCE PERSERVERANCE

To live fully,
To influence many,
To learn daily,
To love without judgment,
To leave a legacy for those that follow,
To think big,
To act on those thoughts,
To help others detect their passion and reach their potential,
To model maturity and wisdom,
To forgive those who have transgressed against me,
To be a "Difference Maker",
To sacrifice for the greater good,
To continue to seek guidance and spirituality,
And to live a life that matters.

### *To live like I was dying!*

As you can see I have four words placed at the top of my mission statement. A good friend and mentor of mine, Bill McEwen, shared those with me one day as part of his mission statement. These are the fuel that drive the car. Everyone needs passion to get where they are going. It rows your boat and helps bring the unwavering desire to see something through to the end. Persistence is the ability to keep going even among opposition, dispirited events, naysayers, and things outside your circle of control that may urge you to stop. Patience must be displayed in all facets of life. God has a plan for each of us but not always on our timetable. Just as nature acts in harmony and on its own time table, so too does the human life cycle. Patience is very much a virtue that must be cultivated. Wherever you are, just remember, be fully present in the moment and understand that everything is exactly as it should be at that time. And finally, perseverance. Perseverance is the emotional intelligence component that is a necessity to be successful in today's fast paced world. It is the ability to bounce back from adversity when you get knocked down, the ability to be self-intrinsically motivated, the ability to be compassionate to others, and the ability to work through challenge to thrive.

Once you have cultivated a mission statement that matters, it is then necessary to live that mission statement. Think about how many times you see a mission statement in an organization that proclaims one thing (such as unmatched customer service) only to get something the exact opposite. If you do this in your own personal life you will create so much static internally that it will limit you from finding your voice in life and will urge you to keep others from finding their voices. This internal turmoil will cause you grief and misalignment with your conscience and will stagnate your life. Mission statements, if produced properly, tap into your heart, mind, and soul and should be sacred documents that tie thoughts with actions. If you produced this document it makes an imprint in your brain and helps you make it legitimate in your heart. As you live from your mission you are connecting what you feel is important to the many challenges of your life. As seen earlier, this is how a translation of this event looks:

**Figure 7. Building Capacity**

# Building Capacity

## Translating the Mission to the Moment

Mission  Moment

## Capacity to Meet Challenges

When you begin connecting the dots from your deeply held beliefs to your daily transactions with others, a deep wellspring of peace and simplicity will take over your life, and you will begin to understand that all people are connected to the same source. Now that you have five important components in place, it's time for an important breakthrough in your life. Something is building inside you, and you are about to experience a powerful awakening.

# 6. Build Up and Breakthrough

As you continue to build the capacity to act through consistent, repetitive actions, you begin to see positive things manifesting in your life. You experience what Jim Collins (2001) noted in *Good to Great* which he called "Build up and Breakthrough." Many times in your life you have probably seen the fruits of your labor because intentional actions manifested positive things in your life. But surprisingly enough, many of the good things in your life are simply a bi-product of a series of good, principle centered decisions that gradually build up over time. This series of good decisions comes from a deep knowing of one's inner self and an awareness and "presencing" that operates inside you when you believe and act in harmony with your deepest core. I have personally experienced this in my own life where good things happened as a result of continuing to practice the belief model of believing, seeing, doing, and reflecting. Reflection in the process is critical to long-term success because it cultivates the self-awareness necessary to change. It is also vitally important to gain momentum with your decisions through acting around your highest priorities. Without execution dreams stay in the concept stage and never come to reality. Many visionaries see grandeur pictures of a better world, a better life, and a better company but fail to execute from those visions. In his book *Presence (2004)*

Peter Senge, et el quote Robert Fritz: "Building the capacity to crystallize a larger intent requires daily practice, working with what he calls structural tension. This 'structural tension' requires crystallizing vision and recognizing present reality and is especially useful in times of stress or daily crises."

As your four dimensions are optimized in the pursuit of greatness you begin to see that you have a deep calling or purpose in life. Senge et el noted, "What matters is engagement in the service of a larger purpose rather than lofty actions that paralyze action." Many times in life we expect success to happen overnight. We see pictures of movie stars that have it all. What we don't see is the road each of them took and where they came from to achieve that level of success. The real success is in the doing, in the journey, and in the acting around one's priorities. As you move in the direction of your dreams with intention, that very intention will co-create your reality. Begin building up today because you are well on your way to a breakthrough soon. Now it is time to create the ultimate mission statement, "Live like you were dying."

# 7. Live Like You Were Dying

When you create a mission statement, it needs to become a powerful, living document that is a personal constitution for how you really want to live your life. Too often we simply allow others to define us, allow circumstances to control us, or we disempower ourselves and allow the world to hold us hostage. We have forgotten how to dream and take control of our lives, our time, our energy, and our future. As we become older we begin to understand that time is the most precious commodity we will ever have. We cherish the little things, forget the silly things, and seek to serve and uplift others. We answer a calling to a higher purpose and we see the beauty in virtually everything we do, even the adversity.

Just last year one of my favorite singers Tim McGraw released the song, "Live Like You were Dying." Many people have made that statement many times but in that particular context it made perfect sense to me. I begin to close my speaking engagements by challenging everyone to value every second, every minute, every hour, and every day in an upward spiral of service, meaning, and contribution. I challenged everyone, in essence, to live like they were dying. Today, for you it may be to let go of some hurt you've harbored, forgive someone who has transgressed against you, quit allowing the past to hold your future hostage, quit allowing others to define who you are and what you stand for, quit the job you hate, tell the one you love, be there for someone that needs you, enjoy a moment of peace, practice spirituality, or just make a conscious choice to be thankful, humble, and happy.

I specifically don't know where you are on your journey, but I will assume yours is not that much different than mine, full of hope, passion, dreams, sorrow, joy, and abundant opportunity. What you PERSONALLY decide to do between your stimulus and response will make all the difference in the world as it relates to you living a life that matters. From my perspective, the most powerful mission statement in the world is to "live like you were dying."

# Chapter 7 Summary—
# Seven Action Items to Manifest the Key Act Up

1. *Today*, I will fully understand that between stimulus (what happens to me) and my response (how I choose to respond) is a space, and in that space lies my ability to choose my response. Today, I will accept full responsibility for how I feel, what I think, how I choose to act, and what I do. Today, I will build the important capacity and overcome the hardwire of my past and the cultural software of my present and seek to become a person of trustworthiness, influence, change, and positive energy. Today, I will manage my energy and place it in areas that leverage my talents and passions and has the most dramatic impact on society and my organization.

2. *Today*, I will fully understand that building internal strength is just like building external strength. Today, I will lift the internal weights of making and keeping

my commitments to my self and to others. Today, I will educate and obey my conscience by living a principle-centered life. Today, I will act in my moments of choice to translate my mission to the daily tough points of my life. Today, I will seek to create a synergy between my walk and my talk and will act in congruence with my true inner self. Today, I will practice abundance versus scarcity and be genuinely pleased for the success of others. Today, I will not say a negative word about another behind their back and will practice patience and humility. Today, I will build versus destroy.

3. *Today*, I will practice the human endowment of self-awareness to identify my personal roadblocks in my life. I will re-imagine, re-create, and re-connect with who I am and where I want to go. Today, there will be no mistaken identity of my true character because I will seek to illuminate the good in others by what I radiate. Today, I will recognize the six emotional cancers of comparing, contending, competing, criticizing, complaining, and complacency. Today, I will build a strong internal immune system by not participating or allowing any emotional cancer to spread in me or throughout my organization. Today, I will be light, not a judge, a model, not a critic. Today, I will overcome each perceived roadblock I have and work daily to grow, expand, and mature.

4. *Today*, I will ask this question, "What one action can I take today with a singleness of purpose and intention that will leverage the most return on investment and will have the most positive impact on me and the organizations I associate with?" Today, I will seek to build the twenty emotional pushups so I garner the internal strength to meet the external challenges. Today, I will place my time and my energy in causes and people I deem worthy and will seek to leave this world and the people in it better than I found it. Today, I will focus on my circle of influence to grow that circle and will start small and achievable. Every step I take will be taken in the direction of my dreams. Today, I will believe in my self and in my causes and will seek to improve both.

5. *Today*, I will translate my mission to the moments of my life. Today, I will seek to live inspired by tapping into my natural birth gifts of body, mind, heart, and spirit. Today, I will live in congruence with my mission in life and will work to embody goodness. Today, I will not allow my environment or what others might think of me to define who I am or what I do. Today, I will build the internal security to act in my tough moments of my private life. Today, I will seek to win the private battles of my life so I can win the public battles. Today, I will become the change I seek to create in the world.

6. *Today*, I will understand that momentum is my friend and companion. I will work to create momentum in all phases of my life. Today, I will work with a purpose, fervor, intention, and passion toward a worthy cause that I believe in. Today, I will no longer put off until tomorrow what I could do today. Today, I will act between my stimulus and response. Today, I will continue to build knowing that the more I build the more I will receive. Today, I will detach myself from outcomes and will only focus on the process knowing that outcomes will take care of themselves. Today, I will think and act in new ways to achieve new levels of success and significance.

7. *Today*, I will live like I am dying. Today, I will value life. Today, I will value people. Today, I will use my God-given talents to enrich the world. Today, I will lose myself in service to others. Today, I will laugh, smile, sing, dance, listen, help, restore, re-connect, rejuvenize, re-imagine, and practice renewal in my life. Today, I will work in all dimensions to grow myself and others. Today, I will become the person I sat out to become. Today, I will wake up, dream up, clean up, listen up, pay up, build up, and ACT UP.

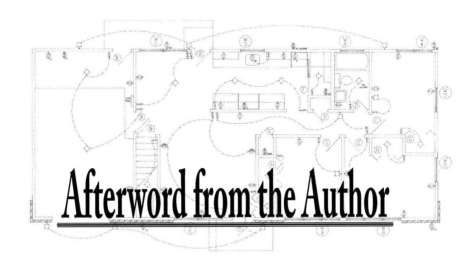

# Afterword from the Author

The journey of completing this book began over three years ago. It speaks to the power of manifestation in your life when you have something so strong on the inside that seeks so desperately to come out. In essence, the beginning of this journey signified the beginning point of my finding my voice in life and working to inspire others to find their voices. The seeds of this book were planted one day while speaking in a college class at Middle Tennessee State University (where I earned my first two degrees) when it came to me what I really wanted to say. That day I begin to call my topic, *"This Ain't No Practice Life."* Deep within each of us is a longing to matter, to contribute, to execute, and to be involved in moving the world forward. Sometimes we become reactive, fail to recognize how our contribution matters, lose our voice, or become frustrated with the process, so we just stay where we are. In reality there is no just staying where we are. We either focus on the solution or we become part of the problem.

By staying we are actively participating in the mediocrity of the world. As Gandhi stated, "We must become the change we seek to create in the world." The *seven keys* that I have put together are just common sense, but not always common practice. They will help you work in a sequential, integrated process toward improving your quality of life, both personally and professionally. The enormous growth that has taken place inside me as a result of sharing this message with literally thousands of people across the United States has been profound. I believe with all of my heart that they will help you start the process of living a life of passionate execution and significant contribution through purpose, passion, presence, focus, and intention. Each step of the way I have illustrated how they have affected me personally to show you that it is possible with everyone.

Dr. Wayne Dyer (2004) in *The Power of Intention* noted that as he sat to write daily that the words came to him from his source or his connection to spirit. I did not fully understand that process until I wrote this book. It emanated from my deepest being and my connection to my spirit. There is a strong push for spiritual intelligence in mainstream America today. To me, this is illustrated through the "whole-person" paradigm of body, mind, heart, and spirit that fills these pages. To work toward your own self-actualization and then to self-transcendence, you must first find your voice in life by waking up and dreaming up. This will be followed with sequential processes of cleaning up, listening up, and paying up. Once you are there you will then build others up around action and execution daily.

My goal for you is simple-live an inspired life and search to create everyday greatness. Deep within each of us is the seed of uniqueness. We are charged with the responsibility of finding and detecting our contribution to the particular needs of the world, and then fulfilling that need with our talent and passion, as driven by conscience. God bless each and every one for taking this journey. My heart goes out to all of those have accepted the fact that *This Ain't No Practice Life*.

Now, go make the world a better place!

*Micheal J. Burt*

# Bibliography

Bennett-Goleman, T. (2001). Emotional alchemy. New York: Three Rivers Press.

Chopra, D. (1994). Seven spiritual laws of success. Amber-Allen Publishing.

Collins, J. (2001). Good to great. San Francisco: Harper Collins.

Covey, S. (1989). The 7 habits of highly effective people. New York: Simon and Shuster.

Covey, S. (2004). The 8th habit. From effectiveness to greatness. New York: Fireside.

Dyer, W. (2004). The power of intention. Georgia: Hay House, Inc.

Frankl, V. (1997). Man's search for meaning. Massachusetts: Beacon Press.

Friedman, T. (2006). The world is flat. New York: Farrar, Straus, and Giroux.

Kouzes, J. & Posner, B. (2002). The leadership challenge. San Francisco: John Wiley and Sons.

Kuhn, T. (1962). The structure of scientific revolutions. University of Chicago Press.

Mackay, H. (2004). We got fired"... and it's the best thing that ever happened to us. New York: Ballantine Books.

Mandino, Og. (1968). The Greatest Salesman in the World. Florida: Frederick Fell Publishers, Inc.

Maxwell, John C. (2000). Developing the leader within you. Tennessee: Thomas Nelson.

Senge, P. (2004). Presence. Massachusetts: The Society for Organizational Learning, Inc.